Praise for *Tea and Cake with Demons*

"In a voice both vulnerable and erudite, balancing storytelling and philosophy, Adreanna Limbach illuminates how to bring the demons of our unworthy feelings along with us on the spiritual journey. Limbach [shares] her own journey in a way that is both disarming and inviting. A lovely book for anybody who wants to get real about the path of awakening."

ETHAN NICHTERN
author of *The Road Home: A Contemporary Exploration of the Buddhist Path*

"Adreanna has written an articulate, respectfully irreverent book that brings essential Buddhist teachings to bear on an obstacle with which we all struggle: insufficiency. If you've felt even for one moment that you aren't enough, this book holds the keys to unlocking greater self-love and abiding acceptance."

ELENA BROWER
bestselling author of *Practice You* and *Art of Attention*

"Whether you're new to meditation or have a lifelong practice, *Tea and Cake with Demons* offers the most crucial teaching to remain right here in the present moment: our worth is unconditional. Through relatable and illuminating stories, and with clear, practical meditations, Limbach invites us to practice this awareness of our inherent worth and change our life in the process."

MEGGAN WATTERSON
author of *How to Love Yourself (and Sometimes Other People)* and *Mary Magdalene Revealed*

TEA

AND

CAKE

WITH

DEMONS

TEA
AND
CAKE
WITH
DEMONS

A Buddhist Guide to Feeling Worthy

ADREANNA LIMBACH

 **sounds true**
BOULDER, COLORADO

Sounds True
Boulder, CO 80306

Published 2019

Cover design and cover image by Rachael Murray
Book design by Beth Skelley

Printed in Canada

Library of Congress Cataloging-in-Publication Data

Names: Limbach, Adreanna, author.
Title: Tea and cake with demons : a Buddhist guide to feeling worthy /
    Adreanna Limbach.
Description: Boulder, CO : Sounds True, 2019. | Includes
    bibliographical references.
Identifiers: LCCN 2018051497 (print) | LCCN 2019015019 (ebook) |
    ISBN 9781683641230 (ebook) | ISBN 9781683641223 (pbk.)
Subjects: LCSH: Eightfold Path. | Four Noble Truths. | Self-esteem—
    Religious aspects—Buddhism.
Classification: LCC BQ4320 (ebook) | LCC BQ4320 .L56 2019 (print) |
    DDC 294.3/444—dc23
LC record available at https://lccn.loc.gov/2018051497

10 9 8 7 6 5 4 3 2 1

For Isabelle

Contents

PART 3 The Eightfold Path

Foreword

One of my favorite stories of the Buddha's path to liberation is about the moments just before he attained enlightenment. He had tried all the spiritual practices of his day: yogic disciplines, extreme asceticism, and abandoning all trappings of conventional life to wander with a begging bowl. He learned many things along the way, but the moment of complete transcendence eluded him. One day he decided to simply sit under a tree in meditation, release all striving, and not move until enlightenment dawned.

During his sit, many demons came to visit him to create disruptions each time enlightenment was near. They made cacophonous noises. They sent cadres of dancing girls. They created horrible odors. (Personally, that's the one that would really throw me.) Nothing worked. They began to taunt him to try and shame him off the path (with sentiments you may be familiar with): *Who do you think you are? You're just a dude, nothing special about you. What makes you think you're worthy?* In a last-ditch effort to dissuade him, the demons resorted to violence and shot arrows at him. But the Buddha's presence was such that, before it could reach him, each arrow turned into a flower and fell at his feet.

I've often wondered about this last bit. What is powerful enough to turn a violent weapon into a flower while you simply sit at your ease? What is it that neutralizes the poisons of desperation, anger, and fear and transforms them into objects of beauty?

Adreanna Limbach's brilliant, beautiful — I love it — new book contains answers to these questions. She presents classical Buddhist teachings in an utterly modern context, without — and this is the key — watering anything down at all or attempting to obscure the power of this mighty spiritual path by couching it in the language of science or psychology. She offers an in-depth look at the foundational teachings — the Four Noble Truths (which include the Eightfold Path) — and the practice of sitting meditation in such a way that you will be able to stay the course of your particular path, quiet shame once and for all, and calm the inner critic, who is constantly shooting judgment at you, not by countering it with superior logic, but by actually making friends with it. In so doing, it turns into your fiercest ally. Rather than attacking you, it will adorn your path with flowers.

Susan Piver

Introduction

There is a widely circulated Buddhist story about the time that a demon came to town and everyone lost their minds. This wasn't any garden-variety demon, mind you, and yes, there are garden-variety demons. A touch of awkwardness, restlessness, longing—anything that nibbles at our peace of mind can be considered a demon; albeit some are harmless and benign. These are the basic sorts of demons that we meet any old Monday afternoon when we're pinged with the impulse to be somewhere else or somebody else or to just go grab a snack out of boredom. This particular demon story, however, is about Mara, who in Buddhist cosmology is the most malignant demon of all. You might recognize Mara if you saw him, but if he's a pervasive force in your life, then in the same way that we can develop an acclimated blindness to what is overly familiar, you might not see him at all. Mara is the specter of delusion whom we chauffeur through our life; the interior voice that robs us of our faith, trust, and confidence, of our belief that we are fundamentally whole. In Buddhist mythology, Mara is self-doubt personified; a force that's depicted as convincing, relentless, and strategic, and in this story he's coming for the Buddha.

Buddha's attendants caught wind that Mara had materialized, and they went running to alert Buddha that his nemesis was near. In my own paraphrased version, I imagine a cohort of visibly shaken monks clad in saffron robes banging on the

Buddha's door. "Buddha! Buddha! Mara is here! Mara is here!" When the Buddha opened the door to his distressed attendants, they understandably launched into strategy. "What should we do? Should we run? Let's pack up our begging bowls and get out of town. We have enough advance warning that we can probably outrun him!" Another monk chimed in, "We'll never be able to run fast enough. Let's hide! I know of a place that is secure and hidden. Mara will never find us there. Quick!" Yet another chimed in, "Maybe we should plan an ambush! Let's arm ourselves with shields and spears and face Mara on the offensive!"

This part of the story I relate to deeply. It's as though these monks are diplomats of my own mind. More than a decade of meditation practice has afforded me many hours of watching my relationship to discomfort. The moment I feel it, I'm on the express track to strategizing my way out of it. This reaction applies to even the most mundane experiences. The absence of air-conditioning in August. An awkward conversation. A mosquito in my vicinity. Never mind how I might react if Mara, the Lord of Delusion, rolled into town with my name in his mouth. Just like the monks, without skipping a beat, my mind launches into *How do I fix this right now?* I don't want to spend time with my discomfort. I certainly don't want to feel it. I just want it to be different. Better . . . with the least amount of effort, if possible.

There is something universal being spoken to in this story of Mara, which is, of course, the enduring beauty of mythology. Each of these monks represents our habitual ways of reacting when we come into contact with our demons. We want to run from them, or hide, or fight. What the Buddha does instead is so counterintuitive that it offers us a wholly alternative plan of action for when we encounter our demons.

In the presence of his attendants trying to strategize the problem of Mara away, he holds his seat and gives simple instructions: "Go fetch Mara and escort him to my door. Set the table with my finest china. And invite him in for tea, not as my enemy, but as my esteemed guest."

My guess is that you have plenty of experience with your own demons, and that you have a number of strategies that you keep by your proverbial nightstand for dealing with them. I say this because if you are human, there's a good chance that you've had your heart broken or, at the very least, have been deeply disappointed by something that didn't turn out the way that you had hoped. There is the classic heartbreak of lost romance or unrequited love. There is the deep disappointment of not living up to our own expectations, perhaps failing to fulfill the promises we made to ourselves about what we needed to succeed or survive—promises we probably made when we were much younger. There is the mundane dissatisfaction of feeling restless or out of place. The impulse to find comfort by moving our leg half an inch. The itch we can't quite scratch. The wish to be elsewhere and the certainty that if we just had a different _____ (fill in the blank), our happiness would click into place. There is the paycheck that never quite stretches far enough; the pain of not being accepted, sometimes by others, sometimes by ourselves; and the ceaseless striving to make something just so. There is the exhaustion, and the stress. There are the nights spent not sleeping or the days spent working too hard. There is the divorce. The death. The diagnosis. There are the societal concerns and injustices, oppression and disillusionment. There are all the ways we will not be able to shield our children from the pains of growing up, or shield ourselves from the pains of growing old. This list is incomplete, and of course it's just a skimming of the surface, but I'm sure that you get my point. Our demons thrive here in hardship and heartbreak, injustice and uncertainty. Because we face our demons so often, it's useful to understand how to relate to them in a way that doesn't perpetuate our unhappiness or stir up a sludgy shame spiral that pits us against ourselves and our experience. This is, in part, where this book comes in.

It's worth noting that in stories in which the Buddha is face-to-face with his own demons, namely Mara the Lord of Delusion, they aren't showcased as his enemies, but rather as his venerated nemeses. This nuance tells us something about what our demons are, or what they have the potential to become. Enemies are interchangeable. They are forces who may be hostile to you or that you just plain don't like. But a nemesis holds an enduring post that makes you wonder if the protagonist—that is, you—could exist without them. Take Harry Potter and Lord Voldemort, for example, or the Jedi and the Sith. Each protagonist-antagonist coupling is a single essence halved right down the center to form two contrasting parts. The thin line that divides them makes them antithetical, like synchronized swimmers in opposition. A hero only knows herself as a hero if there is also a villain in the plot. The sun only knows itself as the daylight because of dusk and the rise of the moon.

The same can be said for the Buddha, who represents our capacity to tap into the wakeful, luminous, clear, and present nature that is always available to us. Through meditation practice we can come to know ourselves to be fundamentally whole and the antithesis to Mara, who represents our confusion and self-doubt. The key to the story of the Buddha inviting Mara in for tea is that every step we take toward revealing the ground of our worthiness will unearth all of the demon material that conceals it; wisdom and confusion ride side by side. This isn't a problem. This is clarity. One begets the other. The way that we continue to embody our worth is to understand the paradox of our shadowy bits and to welcome our own confusion when it arises. The practice is in the invitation. We receive our demons and embrace them at the door, knowing we are whole enough to include it all.

This book explores self-worth and all that obscures it through the lens of the traditional Buddhist teachings of the Four Noble Truths. One of the most common struggles that I've both personally experienced and encountered in others in my work is the pervasive feeling of a fundamental flaw, the sense of not being "good enough." We are reminded repeatedly in myriad ways that we need to be smarter, thinner, more attractive, better educated, employed at a higher level, coupled, and then married with great sex and good skin. Forever. Then, and only then, will we access the happiness granted to those who continue to strive. Yet after years of chasing those external goals, a number of us end up disillusioned; boxes are checked, but we're no closer to fulfillment. Or perhaps we simply feel bad about ourselves, as if everyone else has figured it out and gotten their act together but us. It's of very little surprise that we come to doubt our fundamental worth or that we believe we are destined to be chronically two steps behind.

That's where the Buddha's teachings can be exceedingly valuable. There is no dogmatic "do this and you'll be happy forevermore" sort of nonsense in them, but rather they offer a sustainable path of inquiry with which we can make friends with ourselves, regardless of our circumstances, expectations, or achievements. The Four Noble Truths, in particular, are both practical and experiential teachings designed to help us realize that we are okay, complete, and worthy as we are, in a way that can never be diminished. In this book we'll walk through the foundational teachings the Buddha offered through the lens of this realization, while engaging in practices along the way that will help you discover this simple truth for yourself. Each chapter will offer a perspective, a lens through which we can view our self-worth and the demon material that tends to obscure it, as well as a number of "On the Spot Practices" that act as simple checkpoints for us to integrate these teachings into our lives in a moment-to-moment way.

PART 1

Waking Up to Worthiness

How do you measure your worth as a person? Is it through the eyes of others? Through accomplishments and successes? Behavior and contributions? Perhaps you recognize worth as an intangible force that all other success is built upon. When we have it, self-worth can act as a steady base that grounds us confidently in the world. We feel more able to take up space, to share our voice, to be generous without expectation. When we don't have self-worth we spend vast amounts of unconscious effort hustling to secure it. In the first part of this book, we begin by exploring the theory that perhaps our worth, our value, is an inborn state that we all possess—not contingent on external factors. We then take some time to explore the many forces that obscure our worth, by learning to make friends with our own minds. We begin to explore the path of self-worth as a process of continually coming back to ourselves, over and over again, and by taking time to understand who and what we are at a fundamental level.

1

Acorns Know How to Oak

Our intention is to affirm this life, not to bring order
out of chaos nor to suggest improvements in creation,
but simply to wake up to the very life we're living,
which is so excellent once one gets one's mind and
desires out of its way and lets it act of its own accord.

John Cage, *Silence: Lectures and Writings*

Of all of Aristotle's many landmark contributions to Western society, one of the most touching might be the strange Ancient Greek word *entelékheia*. Modernized over time as *entelechy*, it's the combination of the Greek words *ékhō*, which means "to have," and *télos*, which means "wholeness, completion, or fruition." Spun together, entelechy represents that which has wholeness, that which contains its own completion. It's a form of intelligence considered to be constitutional to all life on Earth, the instinct to develop into our fullest expression of ourselves. Acorns know how to "oak" into mighty eight-story trees. Spiders know how to "silk" and spin webs that by weight are stronger than steel. Caterpillars know how to dissolve into liquid and rebuild their bodies with wings.

My husband and I sometimes marvel at what a dog our dog is. He is the essence of dogness in his very being in a way that is so undeniable and complete. Everything he does is an expression of "dogging," as though his very nature is a verb. It's a delight to watch him instinctively dog, and it's simultaneously unremarkable because there is nothing unique about it. Entelechy asserts that there is an intelligence at play in the natural world that often goes uncredited. It is so benign and overt that it's easy to take it for granted. There is this commonplace miracle of life unfolding everywhere that life exists. The miracle is that all things know how to become; we contain our own completeness as well as pure potential.

One of the fundamental teachings in the Mahayana schools of Buddhism is that of Buddha Nature. Depending on the teaching, it is sometimes referred to as basic goodness, luminosity of mind, or *tathāgatagarbha*, which is the Sanskrit word for Buddha-Essence or Buddha-Embryo and the name of the sutra that the teaching of Buddha Nature springs from. This essence is akin to the entelechy of basic wholeness, completeness, and worth that we all possess. Just by virtue of being human. While Buddha Nature may sound lovely and true to some of us, I realize that for others it may be a hard pill to swallow. Much like the nemesis principle discussed in the introduction, opposing forces develop when we recognize contrast. The moment that we cast a light on our inherent worth, its shadow stands out in sharp relief. How can we talk about the basic goodness of humanity when there is evidence to the contrary everywhere? Bombs are being dropped and people are sleeping in boxes and there seems to be a new humanitarian crisis each week, not to mention the tiny infringements on human dignity that we both suffer and inflict regularly. If you doubt that you undermine human dignity on a regular basis, check the number of times a day that you scroll through your smartphone rather than connecting to the person in front of you. It's a tiny but pervasive example that no one I know is exempt from. From the perspective of Buddha Nature, these small infringements, along with the larger ones such as ignorance, hate, and greed, are obscurations: neurotic manifestations of the mind that spring from the tenderest parts of ourselves. The allegory of inviting our demons to tea suggests that we don't ignore this side of our humanity, rather we learn how to work with it. The entirety of the path that we're on leads us back to our inherent wholeness, which is inclusive of our contrast. Human dignity and it's infringements. Our wholeness includes it all.

The principles of basic goodness remind us that we have a birthright of belonging—to the earth and the earth to us. If a dog is inherently dogging at all times, so do we humans keep returning to our humanity and the clear, luminous, awake, and whole embryo of Buddha Nature that we all possess. Our bodies regularly testify to this inheritance of belonging. There is calcium in our teeth, in the seashells of the ocean, in the sedimentary cliffs of Iran and Utah, and in the bones that hold us upright. The intelligence of design to which we belong ensures that absolutely nothing dies without being carefully wrapped in earth, to be deconstructed and cleaned and used to feed life again. Nothing is wasted, nothing is discarded, everything is workable and has a place.

When left to its own devices, life is in service to life is in service to life in an endless playback loop that ensures that life will persist. A cut will instinctively heal itself and our lungs know how to breathe, without ever being asked, and without us needing to know "how." Right now, there are weeds asserting their place in this legacy by pushing their lives up through cracks in the pavement. Even in the nuclear wasteland that is Chernobyl, which people abandoned in the mid-1980s, wildlife populations are flourishing because nature is tenacious and resilient and finds a way even in toxic environments. This wisdom of nature is reflective of our constitution: what we are and what we will always be. Whole and complete with a primordial intelligence that cannot be reduced, only obstructed. We belong to an Earth that bends toward healing. Sometimes we simply forget. It's so easy to do; there are dishes to wash and taxes to pay and customers to serve and gas tanks that need filling. However, even our day-to-day living, in the light of fundamental worth, might be regarded as divine. Nature also reminds us that our life is but a flimsy moment in an eternal expanse, and that whatever intelligence propels us through the world will also dissolve us back into the earth. Until that day we can always feel our primordial wakefulness through the breath, which cycles without ever being asked to do so.

Winners vs. Losers

The issue with a term like "primordial wakefulness" is that we are constantly bombarded with messages that dull us and tell us we aren't good enough. Therein lies the rub. There's a moment when most of us receive the message that we're not quite good enough the way that we are. Perhaps there's a cultural standard that we become aware of, along with the place that we occupy in it. Maybe there's a family dynamic that expects something of us that we find ourselves unable to fulfill. Or a disappointment that's assigned to who we are, rather than something that we did. Perhaps we learned to reject the standard of "good enough" as mediocre, subpar. "Okay" is not actually okay. You have to be the best, or you are nothing. Make it perfect, or don't try. Deep down many of us carry a subtle but nagging distrust of ourselves, or a trust that feels somewhat conditional, requiring fresh proof of concept at every turn. Unable to fully relax, we're always looking over our shoulders for confirmation from the right people that we're actually doing okay in our lives.

The moment I received the message that my worth was conditional was the moment that I realized that we were poor. It was the Christmas of 1992, and my family was homeless again, staying with friends of my mother. My step-dad had been in the military and suffered from chronic physical and mental illness, and so the task of raising me and my three siblings often fell on my mom, who in 1992 was still in her twenties. She did the best that she could with the few social and financial resources that she had; however, her best still involved frequent displacement. There was a lot of moving, occasional homelessness, and, overall, never quite enough of anything to get by on.

I was eleven years old at the time, and although our circumstances weren't much different than they had been throughout most of my childhood, I was beginning to feel differently about our lifestyle. It felt less fluid, adventurous, and bohemian and more like wearing a tight itchy sweater. An uneasy feeling was developing, and I noticed it in the discomfort I felt inviting friends over, in the awkwardness that came with the awareness that there was plenty we didn't have. One of my favorite summers of my life we had lived in a garage, and my mom hung sheets from the ceiling as makeshift walls. At the time, living in a tent constructed of pillows and bedsheets was a kooky and wonderful fantasy. But as time passed, a shift in thinking rattled me when reflecting on those moments. I couldn't put my finger on why, but perhaps it was because I was getting older and had more to compare my experience to. I could look at my classmates and think, *Wait, you have a house with a bedroom that has cable TV? How does this all measure up?*

Our Christmas presents had come from the Salvation Army toy drive that year, which, again, didn't feel especially unique. But in the moment of unwrapping my gift, I remember something clicking into place. I had received a doll who stood about two feet tall, with caramel-colored skin and a Scottish tartan kilt. It was quite obvious to me that this doll was meant for a much younger child. It was the first time that I truly grokked not just our circumstances as a family, which were those of limited means, but what those circumstances meant about me and my position in the world: We are poor people. I am poor. "Poor" is a shameful thing to be. It was the beginning of a deep discomfort with myself that split my world, like cleaving an apple into two halves. There were winners, I reasoned, and there were losers. And we were on the wrong side of the tracks. No one had to tell me this; I had inferred it from social situations and television.

Economically poor folks are frequently portrayed as people who are lacking in dignity. There's the trope of the welfare queen who plays the victim while having babies and working the system, or of the uneducated trailer trash who's too lazy and ignorant to better his life. If you are poor, it's often assumed that you brought your circumstances upon yourself either through so-called stupid life choices, such as self-medicating with drugs or alcohol, or an unwillingness to pull yourself up by the bootstraps. Even the word *poor* is a double entendre. One quick dictionary search reveals it to mean "low income" but also "inadequate," "substandard," "limited," "faulty," "abysmal," and "pathetic." The United States itself was founded by Protestant Calvinists who believed good social and economic fortune was proof that one had God's favor. It's not an unlikely stretch for one to interpret being broke as an external reflection of merit and character.

At eleven years old, I didn't know what an "internalized narrative" was. I just carried a world of shame. In that moment of unwrapping the doll, I decided that I would lie to my friends about what I had gotten for Christmas and do everything in my power to prevent myself from being "found out" as inadequate, substandard, poor. If the world was a binary of winners and losers, then I would make it my mission to be a winner. Ambition that's born from shame and self-loathing is powerful, but unfortunately it's a fuel that doesn't burn clean.

Following the Bread Crumb Trail

You may also have a story like mine, a moment that was formative in your relationship with yourself. Maybe it was a series of moments that slowly eroded your confidence. Perhaps you formed adaptive strategies for letting only the acceptable parts of you show, or, at the very least, strategies to conceal your shame. Me? I overcompensated for my sense of inadequacy and was crowned prom queen my sophomore year of high school. My clothes were right, my hair was right, my friends were right. In the world of winners versus losers, I was determined to come out on top.

This strategy of mine began to unravel my junior year, when I enrolled in a class called A History of Great Ideas. The course's name was just innocuous enough to fly under the radar as an elective at my small-town Midwestern school, but its content was far from benign. It was taught by Mr. Siebert, who was wonderfully weird and charmingly grumpy, both qualities that made me want to study with him. This course offering is how I found myself, at seventeen years old, in my first Buddhist studies class.

I will never forget the feelings of excitement as these brand-new concepts worked their way into my mind. The suggestion that I might be more than my curated persona was like riding the steep drop of a roller coaster; my very young grasp on reality was scrambled into a mass of question marks, and I knew that I wanted to learn more. I launched my meditation practice and was appalled by what an inhospitable home my own mind was for me. It offered a playback loop of nattering shame and perfectionism, of never living up to my own standards, but I persisted.

It wasn't until my midtwenties, however, that my meditation practice truly took root. I was living in New York City, knee-deep in my quarter-life crisis with no idea what I wanted to do with my life. The only thing I knew for sure was that I was definitively not where I thought I should be at that point in life. Single. In debt. Aimless. And then came the panic attacks. I hyperventilated on the subway, and at work, experiencing very public meltdowns. If you've experienced the terror of a panic attack, then you are familiar with the choking sensation of feeling your mind and body cave in. The life implosion I was experiencing externally had somehow manifested in physical form.

Around this time my new roommate began taking Buddhist studies classes at a local nonprofit meditation center called The Interdependence Project. She invited me along, and it was in that first class that something clicked for me. I remembered how helpful these practices had been when I first encountered them, and I committed myself to giving them a real chance. It was a bit like following the bread crumb trail back to my meditation cushion, which I've subsequently been doing in earnest now for the past decade. The proof is in the pudding, as they say, and the shifts in my own relationship to myself and the world at large have been deeply healing and undeniable.

After completing the Buddhist Studies Immersion Training at The Interdependence Project in 2012, I began exploring how so many of us struggle with our own internal demons, the narratives and states of mind that prevent us from trusting that we are inherently worthy of being loved and happy as we are. My work has afforded me the privilege of being in conversation with diverse cross sections of people, and I've found the widespread nature of self-doubt striking, though not necessarily surprising. Though the content of conversations may shift depending on whether I'm hosting an international group coaching program, teaching at a halfway house for women transitioning out of prison, or teaching one of my regular classes at MNDFL meditation studios in New York City, one theme remains the same: deep down we have a nattering voice that questions our basic goodness, our fundamental enoughness. The beauty of the teachings of the Buddha, specifically the teaching that we are innately worthy, is that they are accessible to you where you are, right here at this very moment — which is, in part, what makes them so effective. There's no need to add more to them. With the teachings, we're just following that bread crumb trail back to our capacity for an awake and present mind that within us is already complete.

On the Spot Practice Feel the weight of your body on the ground. Take a deep breath. See if you can relax, even just for a moment, in your own skin. That momentary pause where you're resting in the moment and not critical of yourself—that's basic goodness right there.

2

Meeting Our Demons

We find beauty not in the thing itself but in the
patterns of shadows, the light and the darkness,
that one thing against another creates.

Jun'ichirō Tanizaki, *In Praise of Shadows*

Confession: this book was really difficult to write. And when I say difficult, I mean "crying on the floor while eating a block of cheese and calling my mom" kind of difficult. It was tea and cake with my demons—all day long. As I write this, I'm realizing how instinctual it is to get right down against the ground when the going gets tough. It's as though some primal sense of me knows that refuge can be found here, pressed against the earth. There is a trust beyond logic that the earth will hold me when circumstances are rocking my world, an urge to lower my center of gravity, which makes us more difficult to shake. Finding a lower center of gravity is good advice, whether you're crawling through a burning building, learning to ride a surfboard, or facing demons of self-doubt. In case of turbulence, get low to the earth. Such instinct is the wisdom of the body.

Writing this book meant first wrapping my mind around the fact that someone would actually agree to publish a book written by me. As an introverted child who grew up in a chaotic home, libraries were sacred spaces, and books were my salvation. They provided a means of escape and community, even if only fictional, and the realization that I would be adding my stone to the altar by publishing a book was deeply moving. I had a lot of feelings, mostly tenderness and terror. I wanted to do right by a younger version of myself. This took some time to digest.

Then came the realization that this book would always read better in my head than it would on paper because I didn't have the technique to translate it exactly the way that I wanted. This, I've heard, is common among creatives or anyone who has ever set out to do anything that they haven't already done. The gap between one's own good taste and the talent to execute an idea that lives up to that good taste can be wide and treacherous. True demon territory. The trolls that live under the drawbridge between idealism and outcome can and have paralyzed far more talented people than myself, and probably always will. In my case, I had to come around to the grace of setting my standards aside and just writing as well as I could, not as well as I wanted. Being gentle with myself is hard sometimes. So is taking my own advice.

Next came the unexpected—but in hindsight, obvious—occurrence. Writing a book on feeling worthy brought every single ounce of self-doubt I have to the surface. Did I mention the part where I laid on the floor crying and eating cheese? The wonderful thing about having a meditation practice is that I'm able to watch my neurosis with acute awareness. Yes, meditation has made me more settled, sane, and resourceful overall when it comes to dealing with strong emotions. Again, get close to the earth in case of turbulence. Finding my seat in meditation has always provided a sturdy space from which to encounter, understand, and make room for my most crippling bouts of self-doubt. However, I'm sorry to report that meditation has not catapulted me into a blissful realm where only good vibes exist and scary things are no longer scary. That such a place exists is poppycock. I'm still a flawed and neurotic human being like everybody else, with a tendency toward deep sadness, fear, and anger. I have demons in spades. They've just become somewhat less menacing with time, repeated gestures of kindness toward myself, and a stable, grounded base to work from.

I tell you all of this, dear reader, just in case you thought that I was somehow in a vaunted position of "teacher" or "author" with strategies that I would benevolently dispense to radically raise your life a level or two. This is not the case at all. In fact, if this is what you want or expect, then my intention here is to disappoint you right off the bat so that we can enter this book together at eye level, feet on the earth, with a lower, more stable center of gravity. I'm still shoveling my manure, as they say, and probably always will be. You probably always will be too. And that's the good news, because it means that you're meeting your life as it is. Which, if you are human, also includes some demons.

Hello Nasty

For each of us, this demon material is like our own unique neurotic thumbprint. It's in our difficult emotions, confused states of mind, and the unintegrated aspects of ourselves that cloud our Buddha Nature. Historically I've harbored hair-trigger anger that tends to manifest as depression or rage, depending on the chosen target. You might be prone to anxiety or shame, or have different demons altogether that disrupt your daily peace. What comes bounding to the forefront in moments of stress when your natural wakefulness is obscured? This is a pretty good indicator of what your demon material is composed of. Like poking a sleeping bear, our demons tend to rise to the surface when we feel vulnerable, threatened, or hurt.

Some years ago, I was taking my seat at the front of a meditation class that had been booked for a private event. The room was buzzing and chatty with all of the women in attendance talking among themselves at a high frequency. It reminded me of the way that parties or large dinners can pick up volume fast, voices pole-vaulting over each other. As I took my seat, no one seemed to understand that class was beginning. The clamor among participants continued. A few women looked at me and then turned back to their conversation. I politely rang the bell, and many kept talking as I contemplated the most skillful way to gather their attention. Should I clap my hands like a camp counselor? Should I stand back up and raise my voice to greet them? A cocktail waitress who had worked at a raucous nightclub once told me that she was able to cut through the wall of noise by speaking low and softly to her patrons. As I considered her method, and the lovely metaphor of how softness can cut through noise, one woman laughed from the back of the room, "Yeah. Good luck getting us to meditate!" At that point a dagger cut through my mind: *I don't give a fuck if you meditate, Linda. Your participation here is not my job.* I suddenly found the whole situation absurd and her response inconsiderate, akin to walking into a Pilates class and snorting, "Yeah. Good luck getting me to exercise! I just paid $20, but I'm gonna lie on the floor and watch Netflix on my phone unless you can convince me that I should do otherwise!" *Hello, my righteous indignation. Hello, hot and nasty self-importance.* I'm not a big fan of being treated as disposable entertainment or as someone standing between another person and 6:00 p.m. happy hour. But then again, who is? The class had awakened my demons.

I've had students in class like her before. The ones who cross their arms and look at me skeptically, as if to say, "Before I engage, prove to me that this whole meditation thing works." Or the ones who walk into class, take an exaggerated posture with their chests and chins protruding, and request that I make them "Zen." My first thought is often one of irritation, followed by a wave of tenderness. There is the realization that the "good luck getting me to meditate" lady is just declaring her discomfort before anyone else can figure it out. Or that Mister Prove It First probably has a difficult time relaxing into uncertainty and might lean on logic to feel safe. In the same way that my defenses spring to attention when I encounter these types, I'm meeting their defenses as well. Encounters like this have the potential to become one big demon stare-down, in which neither of us is relating to our own fundamental worth, much less to one another's. Underneath our cynicism, self-importance, and flat-out obnoxious behavior, there is often a wiggly, vulnerable part of us that a very old habit is protecting for a very good reason. Of course, as we've been exploring, our defensive qualities are only a fraction of who we are; even if they step forward as our loudest ambassadors, they're not necessarily accurate representatives of us. When we develop an intimate understanding of our own demons, coupled with trust in our fundamental worth, we create the conditions necessary to soften situations by extending this understanding to others. But how do we do this? How have I learned to do this?

One of the great limitations of the English language is that it sets us up to overidentify with the way we feel. In English, we might say "I am angry" to express strong irritation. I can't help but believe that this identification of "I am" informs the way that we think about our feelings and relate to them as a whole. It makes anger, in that moment, the totality of who we are, and sometimes it can seem that way. When I am knee-deep in my demon material, it feels like it has entirely hijacked my identity. Not all languages are like this. The Portuguese *Eu estou com raiva* can be expressed in the same circumstances as "I am angry," but it translates as "I am with anger." I find this to be a sane and workable alternative to "I am angry" when I find myself dealing with situations and people who set my teeth on edge. So when my demons are cavorting, I often think, *I am with my demons right now.* This tweaking of language gives emotions the role of guest and can help us retain the faith that the demons are not the sum total of who we are; they are just passing through. Our defenses, our demons, are not *us* per se, but they do belong to us, which means that they require our supervision and care.

There are a few ways that we traditionally tend to relate to our demons, which is to say, how we tend to avoid them altogether. The first strategy is to chuck them at other people when they feel too painful to hold. It's like a game of emotional hot potato. Anger, annoyance, jealousy, *You take it!* This strategy hews to the old adage that misery loves company. I will toss my demon material at whomever I've decided is the source of my annoyance, or even at innocuous loved ones and bystanders, in an attempt to not face it, or to at least not be with it alone.

The second way that we might tend to relate to our demons is to fixate on figuring them out so that we don't have to feel them or face them in any sort of direct way. This is my personal go-to strategy, because I can analyze anything to a pulp. I have the sense that if I can just put my finger on why I feel a certain way, who else is implicated in the situation, how my reaction probably stems from my childhood, and how I can avoid similar conditions next time, then I have what I'm feeling all figured out, and it's all nice, tidy, and solved. Moving on. "Figuring out" our feelings rather than actually feeling them is just a sophisticated way of bypassing our relationship to our demons altogether. Figuring something out is different from understanding it; it's the difference between creating intellectual distance or developing heartfelt intimacy. Understanding requires time, proximity, and nonjudgmental curiosity.

The third way of habitually relating to our demons is good old-fashioned repression. We swallow whatever is generated in moments of stress and lock it deep down in our inner recesses so that we can go on pretending we're "fine." This strategy is fairly common if we find ourselves in situations and societies where we're not allowed to express certain emotions. In the spirit of being nice, maintaining appearances, or making room to caretake others' emotions, we bury our own feelings and needs. This is the perfect recipe, of course, for growing some seriously shadowy demons, the kind that breed in isolation. When we reject aspects of ourselves that we don't have the space to contain, they do not go away. They simply remain unintegrated, demonized, and tend to cause chaos in the background until they are addressed.

If all of these methods for dealing with demons remind you of the ways the monks wanted to deal with Mara, you're spot on. Like the monks, we also have to deal with the natural human tendency to embody aggression, attachment, and ignorance in their various manifestations. The problem with all three of these strategies is that they drive a wedge between us and our demons, and none of them work long term. It's only by inviting our demons, our confused states of mind, to tea that we are able to truly feel them, understand them, and accept them as both parts of ourselves and as confused little visitors against the backdrop of our inherent wakefulness.

Instead of reacting with these habitual tendencies, I find it useful to address these states of mind directly. When I notice that I'm "with" anxiety, I'll give it some recognition. This often means pausing briefly from whatever I'm doing to call it by its name. *Hello, you prickly little creature, I hope you put the kettle on . . .* Facing a demon can honestly be that simple. Taking a few beats to notice our thoughts, drop into our bodies, and feel the sensation of what we are with creates a friendly dialogue that neither indulges nor represses our demons.

In the case of that raucous meditation class, I was able to pause and notice my irritation. *Hello, old friend. Glad to see you.* By giving it the direct attention and space that it needed to subside, I was able to gather the class and steadily transition us into practice. Often there is some tenderness lurking behind our demon material that just needs a safe space to be felt. Our willingness to befriend our pain and discomfort is how our demon material finds redemption, and in this redemption we find an enduring belief in our wholeness, the kind of wholeness that includes it all.

On the Spot Practice

Take a breath and ask yourself, "How am I feeling, right now?" See if you can stay with any emotion that bubbles up without adding judgment. Just allow yourself a moment, thirty to sixty seconds, to feel the entirety of your emotional state. In this moment, you can recognize that you are not that emotion—it is a part of you for the moment, but it will pass. Don't believe me? Tell me what you were feeling three weeks ago at this time. Are you feeling differently? Reflecting in this way allows you to feel the emotion without saying "I am" that emotion.

3

Basic Botany

You might think of a theory as a toy boat.
To find out whether it floats, you set it on the water.

Stephen Hawking, *A Brief History of Time*

In the fall of 2015, I spent a weekend on retreat with the
Venerable Robina Courtin, an Australian-born Tibetan nun
in the Gelugpa school of Buddhism. Whatever stereotype it is
that you imagine when I say the words "Tibetan Buddhist nun"
(Docile? Meek? Sparse in the personality department?), I assure
you she is the exact opposite. Ven. Robina is sharp of tongue,
quick of mind, and has been known to punctuate her points
with the F-bomb from time to time—shaved head, monastic
robes, and all. In short, she's a real treat, on top of being a
brilliant scholar.

During this particular retreat, one of the participants had
noticed that while we were spending a hefty amount of time
deconstructing the fundamentals of Buddhist view, we weren't
spending much time meditating. And by not much time, I mean
we hadn't meditated at all. This participant rose from his seat
during the Q and A portion of one of Robina's morning talks
and asked why there hadn't been meditation yet. Wasn't that
the whole meat and potatoes of this practice? Wasn't that what
we were here to do? Robina adjusted her robes and leaned in to

face the man. "Well, darling, it's like botany," she said. "Have you ever studied botany?" The participant shook his head no. Meditation, she went on to explain, is fine and nice. One will most likely receive some benefit from it. But meditation without understanding the basics of the view behind meditation is like going to sit outside in your garden without ever having learned the basics of botany. You won't have a framework for knowing what you're looking at. You could, she asserted, sit out there in the garden for hours on end and receive some benefit. However, if you don't know whether you're looking at an herb, a flower, or a poisonous weed, you're doing yourself a disservice. This, her analogy concluded, is the same for meditation practice. Having a basic understanding of the view, or theory that gave birth to meditation practices, can actually give what we're doing on the meditation cushion some context.

It's for this reason that we'll be focusing on both view and practice, practice and view, in this book. The two have a bit of a chicken-and-egg relationship, in that it's difficult to have one without the other. We can think of *view* as the body of teachings that helps us to understand what we encounter when we sit down on the meditation cushion. It is the instruction manual, so to speak, that highlights why and where our demons exist, how to work with our confusion directly, and the process for developing faith in our fundamental worth. View develops our understanding and provides some architecture for our practice.

Practice, on the other hand, is all about taking the view for a spin in the world and seeing how it functions for us as individuals. Butt-on-the-cushion meditation practice is a vital part of practice, as are contemplation, exploration, and bringing the view teachings into relationship with others. Practice is where rubber meets the road, as it were. Practice without view is akin to watching the same load of laundry go around and around over and over again without ever being given the instructions for how to take it out, toss it in the dryer, fold it, and wear it in the world. View without practice can easily become disembodied, analytical, and purely conceptual theory. Without direct experience these teachings can't take root.

Though these teachings are open to translation, knowing that others have been walking this very same path and running the grist through the mill for thousands of years gives me confidence in them. I find this sense of lineage very humbling, and it also boosts my confidence somehow, like the feeling you get looking across a mountain range and feeling both physically tiny and integrated within the vastness. No one made this stuff up; Buddhism isn't a shiny new process, nor is it something that's been branded into oblivion. In fact, it's worth noting that even the Buddha didn't pioneer what he found. The Buddha wasn't a creator, or a God, or an inventor of philosophy. He simply observed the human condition in such granular detail that he was able to organize it as a model that the rest of us could both understand and work with. In the same way that the first mathematicians observed the natural occurrence of quantity and then codified what they perceived as "numbers," and Sir Isaac Newton watched an apple fall to ground and named the force at play "gravity," so, too, did the Buddha observe the natural order of things and organize it as *dharma*, which translates from Sanskrit as "the truth, the way of things, what is so."

I'm asking a few things of you in this book that will help you establish both practice and view. First, I encourage you to investigate how the Buddhist framework relates to you rather than just buying into the view wholesale. If you take one thing away from this book, please let it be this: get dirt under your fingernails. This is the practice piece. True confidence requires sweat equity, and though I'm proposing that your worth is inherent, it can require some effort to reveal and then rest in it. We live in the context of a culture that profits from us believing that we're not enough, which means that most of us have some work to do in order to unearth ourselves from that narrative. This is where meditation and contemplation are indispensable because we get to see this "not enough" narrative at play. Full tilt. No filter.

Second, as you read this book, try to suspend your linear thinking a bit and to adopt a view that's more holistic. This is an element of the view. One of the strongest forces that obscures our worth is the way that we buy into the binary, a dualistic understanding of the world in which extreme thinking flourishes and paradox cannot exist. Something is either good or bad with no room for the in-between. I am suggesting instead that you dip your toes into directional thinking, in which uncertainty, ambiguity, and bothness create a living environment for possibility to exist. For many of us, this is easier said than done. I want to encourage you to just notice when you find yourself clinging to the shores of certainty, and the binary of either/or. Is there space instead for two seemingly conflicting ideas to coexist? This is a fabulous threshold from which to begin practicing a bit of curiosity within your judgment.

The third suggestion that I have is to start studying the spaces where it's hard to like yourself; explore those traits that you find so embarrassing that the potential to accept, forgive, and love yourself here seems foreign or impossible. Notice where self-reproach, shame, and judgment join you at the dinner table. There is a lot of information in the spaces where our demons appear, if we're willing to notice when they surface. Every fable has some sort of fire-breathing monster that guards a vast amount of treasure. Sometimes we need a sword to defeat it. Sometimes we just pour it some tea.

On the Spot Practice

As you end each chapter of this book, take a moment to reflect on this question: Does this teaching mesh with my own direct experience? If not, leave it on the cutting-room floor. If so, contemplate how you might be able to integrate it into the rest of your week.

4

Touching the Earth

All the variety, all the charm,
all the beauty of life is made up of light and shadow.

Leo Tolstoy, *Anna Karenina*

Incidentally, like my own stint with writing this book, the story of the Buddha begins with a breakdown. His origins are also a demon story, as most stories of transformation and triumph are, highlighting how we are made in the perpetual alchemy of falling apart and coming together. Before he was "the Buddha," Prince Siddhartha Gautama was an Indian royal, who I imagine was not unlike the more privileged class of modern Westerners. Buddha simply means "awakened one," or to put it in modern terms, Buddha means "one who is woke." He wasn't a godhead or a mystical being, just a regular person like you and me who developed the capacity to see reality clearly. The only exception is that he lived in a kingdom, unlike most of us. When his mother was pregnant, it was predicted that Siddhartha would become either a great king or a great spiritual leader. His father decided that Siddhartha would follow in his footsteps and join the family business as a great ruler who would vault the kingdom to fame and fortune, as was prophesied. To ensure this fate, the kingdom was sealed off, and Siddhartha was kept within the palace walls—the definition of a sheltered child. He had endless forms of entertainment and beauty, and his every material wish was granted. Inevitably and quite painfully he came to realize that he was living a sterilized reality.

The story goes that on his twenty-ninth birthday, Siddhartha left the palace walls for the very first time. It's at this point that he encountered what are called the Four Sights, his first real taste of the human experience. The first sight was of an old man, hunched over and weathered. When he asked his attendant what was wrong with this man, the prince learned of the truth that we all get old and inevitably lose our youth. The second sight was of a sick person whose body was wracked with disease, which confronted Siddhartha with the truth that all beings are subject to illness and pain. The third sight was of a corpse, Siddhartha's first encounter with death. His attendant explained that death, too, is inevitable, a fate that befalls all living beings. This is old news to you and me, but as you can imagine, Siddhartha was pretty freaked out.

Late in the summer of 2014, there was a funny and touching YouTube video circulating on the internet of a five-year-old named Sadie who had an epic meltdown when she realized that her baby brother was inevitably going to grow up. Through her tears, you could almost see the wormhole of existential panic building as she connected the dots between her brother getting older and the human condition as she wails, "And I don't want to die when I'm a hundred!" There are no historical accounts to verify this theory, but I imagine Siddhartha's first trip outside of his sheltered existence was on par with this type of meltdown. Up until this point, his reality had been a proverbial palace of lollipops and rainbows. He had never been presented with hardship, disappointment, or any opportunity to develop emotional resilience. And when he realized that he, too, would grow old, get sick, experience pain, and die, I imagine his reaction wasn't pretty. So it's not entirely surprising that when Siddhartha encountered the fourth and final sight, he renounced his crown entirely and wandered off into the night. The final sight was that of an ascetic, a wandering sage who had committed his life to the spiritual path of reconciling human suffering.

As was common in the day, the path of the ascetic was one of deprivation, and the practices required denying oneself worldly pleasures, such as clothing, comfort, and frequently, even food. Grueling emotional and physical discipline were considered a mark of advancement. Twenty-six hundred years later, we still see this school of thought alive in the "no pain, no gain" method. In the years that Siddhartha lived as an ascetic, it's said that he tried a number of different practices, as many spiritual seekers do. He'd study with a teacher whom he'd ultimately outgrow before setting off to find another who could assist him on his path.

After a number of years Siddhartha ultimately hit a breaking point. Starving, weary, and no closer to spiritual attainment, he broke his vow of asceticism and took in a bit of food offered by a local townswoman. As he felt his strength coming back, the reformed prince sat underneath the Bodhi tree and vowed not to move from meditation until he witnessed the nature of reality and the origins of human suffering. He devoted himself to awakening.

Naturally, this is where Mara joins the story, the demon of ignorance, the personification of self-doubt and all the resulting afflicted emotions. The clearer and brighter our own wakefulness becomes, the more our shadowy demons snap into view. The same is true for Siddhartha. Mara arrived bent on preventing Siddhartha from attaining enlightenment by showing him all of his demon material. He descended upon the Bodhi tree, where Siddhartha was in meditation, with his three dancing daughters in tow. Representative of all things shiny and delicious, these three beautiful women worked their wiles in an attempt to seduce Siddhartha and break his concentration from the tedious task of enlightenment. However, Siddhartha held his seat, unswayed by the prospect of having a fun time with these lovely ladies, and committed wholeheartedly to waking up to the truth of things. Frustrated that craving wouldn't knock the young prince off of his seat, Mara descended upon the Bodhi tree again with a fierce horde of warlike demons spewing hatred and violence. Siddhartha continued to hold his seat through this hostile assault, and when Mara realized that aggression wouldn't unhinge the young aspirant, he switched tactics again.

At this point, I imagine that most of us would have abandoned ship and left our meditation behind. I've ditched meditation for much less terrifying or tempting reasons. Who needs a demon attack? Sometimes I'm just bored, or tired, or want an afternoon snack. However, Siddhartha held his seat, inviting these demons in. Mara, growing increasingly more frustrated with his inability to prevent Siddhartha's enlightenment, resorted to one final attempt to break his will. For his coup d'état, it's said that the Lord of Delusion brought forth the big guns, his mightiest artillery—the simple challenge of "Who do you think you are?" This question taps into our primal fear that we're not even worth the space we occupy. In some versions of the story, it's said that the army of demons, foiled in their attack, howled in unison to testify to Mara's omniscience. "And who will vouch for you?" Mara spat, questioning Siddhartha's right to awaken. With that, Siddhartha silently touched the earth, which trembled in confirmation. His inherent wholeness, dignity, and worth was reflected back to him, and Siddhartha was enlightened at dawn.

The phrase "learning to hold one's seat" is sometimes used in meditation. Holding one's seat is the practice of finding a vantage point in space, the place where our body rests, the physical space that we occupy. It involves taking a moment to fully arrive. We feel our body on the meditation cushion, and we soften into our shape. There's a felt sense that this is it and that we belong here. Unequivocally. Organically. Without effort or justification. I consider holding my seat on the cushion to be a training ground for learning to take up space in a way that is gracious and gentle, without the aftertaste of bravado or self-protection. There's nothing to protect because there is no one who can take it away. Holding one's seat is a way of occupying space that isn't up for debate or proof of credentials. It just is—a testament to our fundamental belonging. Holding our seat carries a quiet conviction that whatever happens, we will be okay. Whatever arises in meditation, we will meet it. We can take refuge in our inherent worth without allowing our sense of self to get knocked around by our circumstances. As the old Zen saying goes, everything is workable. Nothing is wasted or lost.

When we train in holding our seat on the cushion, we find ourselves more able to hold all of life's challenges when we emerge from meditation with space, sturdiness, courage. Holding our seat is the radical practice of revealing, and then resting, in our fundamental okayness. However, it's easier said than done. Which is why we practice. Siddhartha awakened to his own Buddha Nature, in part, because of his response to Mara. The Lord of Delusion kicked up all of Siddhartha's demon material, including the fundamental question of his worth, but there was no negotiation, no fighting back, no strategy employed. There was only him holding his seat under the Bodhi tree and quietly asking the earth to bear witness. In case of turbulence, lower your center of gravity.

 Train yourself in holding your seat. The next time an email lands in your inbox that deeply triggers you, take three deep breaths and sit with the emotions that arise. Remind yourself that you are okay in this moment. Feel what you feel, and move on to the next item on your to-do list, returning to the email later. With this practice you are learning to not react to everything that comes your way. We can create more space in our life simply by pausing and holding our seat.

5

How to Hold Your Seat

If you've ever wished for a friend who would love you as you are, appreciate your genius, and make space for your foibles, welcome you when you're funny and shiny and when you're a complete mess—well, I can introduce you to this person. Rather, your meditation practice can.

Susan Piver, *Start Here Now*

Sitting down on the meditation cushion for the first time often makes one thing blazingly clear: there is no escape from our own mind. There is a wonderful account of Tibetan meditation master Chögyam Trungpa Rinpoche taking a few weeks to travel for recreation. Upon his return a student asked, "How was your vacation?" to which Chögyam Trungpa responded, "Vacation from what?" The punchline is that no matter where we are, we find ourselves. There's no vacation from being you. The scenery changes, but we have the same habits, wisdom, and neuroses whether we're in our bedrooms or on the beach. This is the good news, even if it's uncomfortable news, because no one, or nothing, can save us from eventually turning and facing ourselves. What we do with what we find when we encounter ourselves is matter of personal responsibility.

Meeting Our Minds as They Are

The Eskimos are said to have fifty different words for *snow* because it's such a prominent part of their landscape. For the same reason there are a number of different words for *meditation* in the Indo-Asiatic languages that we can look to for guidance when we sit down to practice. I deeply connect with the Tibetan word *gom*, which means "to familiarize," and the Pali words *bhavana*, which means "development," and *kammatthana*, which means "the work at hand." Taken together, these translations give us a hint that the work of meditation is to familiarize ourselves with our own landscape, which is how development happens. We're creating space to simply notice without pushing, pulling, or otherwise tinkering to create an experience that matches an agenda. First we rest, and take notice. Any friendship begins by first becoming familiar with the other person. Meditation is where we begin to meet ourselves and develop an awareness of our mind. While meditating we're able to open a door to anything that arises: the wisdom of our inherent wakefulness and the confusion of our demons alike.

Paying attention to the breath is one of the oldest meditation techniques on record—and for good reason. Our breath travels well, so it is always with us. It also anchors us to our body, which, unlike the mind, can only be in one place—right here and right now. The breath is also a changeable and dynamic moving target, much like our life. If we're able to practice steadily resting our attention on something that is in motion in meditation practice, we're more equipped to find steadiness in the ever-changing landscape of our life. As an added, quantifiable bonus, studies have linked attention to breathing (through the nose) to the activation of the parasympathetic nervous system, triggering our body's "relaxation response," a phrase coined by Dr. Herbert Benson, who developed a body of research about this effect at Harvard Medical School in the 1970s.[1]

Breathing meditation is also the type Siddhartha Gautama practiced while sitting under the Bodhi tree. I figure that if meditation was his practice on the path to enlightenment, then what do I have to lose? Again, we don't need to work to manufacture some sort of experience; we're simply centering ourselves in the one that we're having, over and over again. With breathing meditation we're purely meeting our life and our mind as they are—no extra bells or whistles needed. One of the most beautiful auxiliary benefits of bringing our attention to our breathing—gently and consistently—is that it's also a practice in simplicity. We're reminding ourselves that this is it. Just one thing. The breath in the body. Given how busy and cluttered our lives often are, a little bit of simplicity practice can go a long way toward staving off the internal overwhelm many of us feel.

If you've tried meditation and you feel like you can't quite figure the whole thing out, my bet is that you're probably better at it than you think you are. Because we're so used to judging our experience on the binary of good/bad, pass/fail, it makes sense that we would see our experience of meditation the same way. This is why meditation is the perfect practice for beginning to bend the binary a bit. Are there pockets where you can rest with your experience as it is, no judgment?

I tell my students that there is no "good" meditation or "bad" meditation—even if your mind was running seventy-five miles per hour and you never found your breath, it wasn't bad. There is, however, *effective* meditation, and the marker of effective meditation is if you are able to come back and report on what the experience was like for you or what you noticed. If you can do this, it means that you were there with the meditation, even if for only a moment. So if you feel like you can't quite figure meditation out, this self-doubt tells me that you noticed something, even if it's just that meditation practice is difficult. That's great. Your mind is busy. No big deal. Try it again. Your time on the cushion is time well spent, I promise.

SHAMATHA
Mindfulness of Breath Meditation

I'm going to introduce you to shamatha meditation in which we focus on the breath. *Shamatha* is the Sanskrit word for "calm abiding," which is more colloquially referred to as mindfulness of breath. I recommend that my students meditate daily; meditation practice is a little bit like brushing one's teeth—that fresh feeling only lasts for so long, and then it starts to get a little gnarly in there. I've found it beneficial to practice for short periods every day rather than for an hour and a half once a week. Regardless of how you approach meditation, it's key to not be too hard on yourself if you skip a session. Self-aggression is counterproductive. Ten minutes is a really great place to start, and then incrementally bump the time up every two weeks or so: ten minutes daily, and then fifteen, and then twenty. It sounds silly, but committing fully to the exact same amount of time every day trains our mind to relax into that time frame. Shamatha meditation is a quintessential practice and the baseline for all of the practices in this book that follow. Here's a set of instructions to get you started:

- Begin by finding a comfortable seat, which can be a formal meditation cushion or a chair. There are no rules, so long as your body is upright and in a position that feels sustainable. If you're seated on a chair, it can be useful to scoot to the front edge to ensure that your feet are planted firmly on the earth and the body is alert and upright.

- Find the points of posture that indicate your body is supported and stable with sustainable physical alignment. It might be worth propping your seat up so that the hips are slightly higher than the knees, and there is some length in the hip flexors between the hips and the thighs to ensure circulation through the legs. You might rock back and forth gently on the cushion or chair to find your sitting bones nuzzling into the surface beneath you. These bony little knobs at the base of your pelvis are often located much farther down than we anticipate, near the crease where your tush meets the thigh. Resting the weight of your body on the sitting bones rather than back on the tailbone will be nicer on your back over time. Walking your attention up your spine, you can feel the vertical stacking of your spine lifting lightly upward. You might rock your head back and forth gently on its axis to locate that natural point where the head rests atop the spine. When your body feels upright, effortless, and sturdy, you'll know you've found that natural plumb line of gravity through the body. This position allows the weight of gravity to pour down through the bones, connecting the body to the earth without the muscles or tendons doing any of the work to hold you.

- Eyes can be open, with your gaze cast loosely downward to a point a few feet in front of you. If it's within your practice to keep the eyes closed, challenge yourself to stay alert and awake so that you don't just doze off into nap time or space out. Taking a few moments to open up your practice, you can begin by feeling your body here in space in a very specific way. Allow the full weight of the body to rest against the chair or meditation cushion, this representation of earth below you. Feel into the points of pressure where the body makes contact. Experience the shape that the body makes, the temperature of the air that's been displaced around you, the texture of your clothing on your skin. There is very little effort needed here. You're simply arriving here fully by receiving the environment and feeling into your body.

- Moving your attention toward your breathing, it might be worth noting where the breath feels most present in the body today. Perhaps it's the vacillation of warm and cool air at the tip of the nose. Perhaps it's the rise and fall of the belly with the breath. You can spend a few moments here just acquainting yourself with the simple sensation of how your breath moves through your body today. Allow your attention to ride the cycle of breath as it moves through your body. There is very little effort needed here. No need to alter or control your breath. Just feeling its natural expression.

- Wherever the breath feels most available in the body today, take a moment to consciously drop an anchor of attention here, marking this the home base of your practice. Continue to practice by working with the simple instruction that as your mind (naturally) begins to wander, notice when you've left your breathing, acknowledge what captures your attention, and then very gently but firmly come back to the sensation of breathing. You can continue to practice in this way for however much time you allotted yourself.

Remember, returning to the breath is truly a practice of returning back home to yourself over and over again. When you drift, it's no big deal. The practice resides in the ebb and flow of releasing and returning. When you find yourself drifting, you can acknowledge where you land, feel your body resting in space, and then feel your way back to your breath inside your body. Shamatha meditation is a practice of continual return.

On the Spot Practice Launch your meditation practice. Start with ten minutes, right now. Read the instructions above, put down the book, and let today be the first day of the rest of your life of practice.

PART 2

The Four Noble Truths

In a nutshell, the Four Noble Truths are teachings on human dissatisfaction and how to go about finding our way out of this dissatisfaction. Informally we might call them "the path of getting our act together and learning to love ourselves more along the way." The teachings themselves have been worked and refined over centuries, poured into the containers of different cultures while absorbing the distinct flavors of each, and yet they remain the cornerstone of the Buddha's teachings, regardless of culture or tradition.

The First Noble Truth is the Truth of human dissatisfaction. With this teaching we investigate the bummer of being a human on a comprehensive scale, ranging from boredom to anguish, and the distinct ways that this dissatisfaction manifests for us. The Second Noble Truth, the Truth of the cause of suffering, sheds some light on our situation by sharing the causes of dissatisfaction; it's a pragmatic reminder that if dissatisfaction exists, then there must be a reason why. With this teaching we come face-to-face with the wellspring of our demons in an effort to understand them. The Third Noble Truth is the Truth of cessation—that there is a way to stop the cycle of delusion and to take heart in our inherent worth, and the teachings can help us. The Fourth Noble Truth, which is the Truth of the Eightfold Path of practice, is where the rubber meets the road, giving us practical guidance on how to live a life based in self-worth.

6

Restless Everything Syndrome

The First Noble Truth

> It is almost banal to say so yet it needs to be
> stressed continually: all is creation, all is change,
> all is flux, all is metamorphosis.
> Henry Miller, *Sunday After the War*

Here is the First Noble Truth: it is hard to be a human. The more that you love, the more you will inevitably lose, and this is the trade-off to living a full life. Injustice abounds. It will be difficult to rest in your own skin at times. And everything will change. Even your skin itself will change, from taut and dewy to wrinkled and worn. This is if you are lucky enough to make it that far. There is no guarantee that you will. No one and nothing can save you from the difficulty of being human. We all experience it. This is not good news or bad news. This is just the news—basic and primary to our existence. And this is where we begin with the Four Noble Truths.

I don't know why, exactly, we begin with suffering on the Buddhist path, though I find it refreshing. Perhaps we start here because dissatisfaction gives us easy entrée into the human experience. There are a thousand different preferred compositions of pleasure, but pain is distinctly universal. It may also be because heartbreak has the unique potential to open us up; sadness makes people tender and malleable before it hardens into resentment or anger. The experience of our own vulnerability offers us unique accessibility to our heart. Perhaps we find ourselves beginning here because it's natural to enter a state of seeking when we've experienced loss. We often feel an urge to heal the gap left by our losses, which leads us to the meditation cushion, the yoga mat, the chapel, or our knees. We get close to the earth in times of trouble. In any case, we don't begin with joy. We start by directly experiencing our dissatisfaction.

The Truth of Dukkha is the Buddha's first teaching. *Dukkha* is a Sanskrit word commonly translated as "suffering." Maybe it's my juvenile sense of humor kicking in, but *dukkha* has always sounded appropriate for what it represents—like something you step in and get on your shoe. You try to wipe dukkha off in the grass, but the smell still follows you wherever you go. Dukkha is the cow pie of daily life, or, as the great Tibetan teacher Chögyam Trungpa once wrote, the "manure of our experience."[1] If you find yourself looking around you and thinking *I'm definitely not suffering*, I applaud you for recognizing your privilege. You probably have running water, food to eat, and a warm home to come back to at the end of the day, possibly in a place that isn't currently experiencing war. Maybe you were born into a body that grants you unseen advantages, either by gender, skin tone, or ability. Perhaps your religion or sexual preference fits neatly into the dominant social narrative. You may even have the accoutrements that make living especially sweet, such as a warm someone to cuddle with and count on when it matters, an unlimited yoga membership, and a stable income. Right now as I write this, I have a puppy curled up at my feet and a soy latte within hand's reach, and my life does not resemble the common definition of suffering at all. I have a whole lot of those "favorable" boxes checked.

Except there is also a subtle draft in my apartment that I wish I had gotten fixed before winter. And my foot has fallen asleep because of the pressure of the dog on it. I'm also wondering, as I'm writing, if this is a total waste of time, and if this book will ever see the light of day. And, if by some miracle this book does get published, and you by some miracle are reading it, I'm worried that you won't find it useful and might just think that I'm a hack. Because am I really qualified? There are plenty of people who have studied longer and could write this better. I'm terrified that I'm just going to reveal all my blind spots to the public, and people will post poop emojis next to my work on social media. I'm feeling a little panicked about my deadline. Also, now my latte is gone. I wish I had ordered a grande. I wonder what's happening on Instagram . . . Maybe someone "liked" a post of mine . . .

This is how suffering, or dukkha, works; it's really that insidious. Everything might be surface-level fine, and maybe even big-picture great, but there's always a hint of dissatisfaction, followed by an impulse to distract ourselves—quickly. Sometimes dissatisfaction is not readily apparent, but if we look closely enough, we can catch it just from the corner of our eye. I have a friend who describes the demon of her self-doubt, a familiar form of dukkha, as a weird little pervert who's always lurking around the corner, ready to distort the way she sees things. I find this description spot on for my own self-doubt. One moment I'm feeling good, and the next moment my doubt comes creeping out from behind a corner with a '70s porn mustache and an open trench coat to remind me of how self-conscious I should be. I also appreciate this description because it reminds me not to take my self-doubt so seriously.

It's just a pervy little demon representing the Truth of Dukkha and asking for my attention.

The thing about dukkha, or suffering, is that it comprises an expansive palette of shades of gray. Like most things in life, there are no absolutes with dissatisfaction, just shades of it on a spectrum of experience. When I was studying color theory as a costume design major, I became obsessed with the nuances of color. Previously, I had considered orange to be orange and gray to be gray. There was dark and light gray, obviously, but upon closer inspection with a trained and guided eye—Revelation! I was able to see that there really was a difference between tangerine and apricot, battleship gray and gunmetal. There are 256 different shades of gray that the eye can discern, and my education opened up an entire spectrum to me that I had previously been oblivious to, simply because I didn't know how to look at what I was looking at.

The same is true of our varying experiences of dissatisfaction. There is suffering in the way we traditionally consider it—desperation, panic, or lying immobilized by anguish, sobbing in a pile of dirty laundry after everything falls apart. (Check!) And then there are the more subtle forms of suffering—impatience, annoyance, a late train on a rainy morning, or the mold on the cauliflower that you wanted to eat for lunch. This type of suffering won't traumatize you, or even linger in your mind, but it is an understated shade of dukkha in which our garden-variety demons show up in their casual daywear, demanding to be seen.

The Three Styles of Suffering

"Suffering of suffering," the first type of dukkha that the Buddha spoke about, refers to the obvious dissatisfaction of painful experiences and generally not getting what we want. This is the style of suffering that we can point to and rather easily agree is pain, such as stubbing your toe. From the moment we're born, we are put in situations in which we don't quite get the flavor that we ordered, and, frankly, it's a bummer. I can't remember being born, but I don't imagine the process was exactly fun—for either party involved. The womb seems like it would be a warm, cozy, quiet, and safe place where everything is provided for. I imagine being there was like living in a pillow fort that has takeout on demand. Then came the moment when, without choice or volition, we were forcibly pushed out of our home through a very small opening into bright lights, oxygen, and chaos. From that moment on, we've experienced tremendous joy and beauty in life, but also disappointment and pain. This is part of the gig. We get sick. We get injured. Our fragile bodies eventually fail. Zen master Shunryu Suzuki suggested that life is like stepping onto a boat that is about to sail out to sea and sink. For me, this is an overarching lesson of the suffering of suffering.

No matter how many buffer zones we build between ourselves and our heartbreak, no matter how strategically we plan to have the exact experience we want, suffering of suffering says, "Fat chance, sweetheart." We will experience physical pain because we interface with the laws of nature and have temporary, vulnerable bodies. We will experience emotional and mental pain because we have needs, such as love, safety, and belonging, that at times will feel challenged, or unstable. Sometimes these needs are deeply tied to a person or a collective that fails us, leaving us with shaky bearings and an even shakier sense of identity. We can point to this type of heartbreak and easily identify it as painful. We didn't get what we wanted. In fact, we got exactly what we had hoped to avoid.

The second type of dukkha is the "dissatisfaction of impermanence" and refers to the pain of loss. This dissatisfaction is the painful truth that life is perpetually changing, and we can't do anything about it. A few days before writing this section, I passed by a row of freshly cut Christmas trees propped up against a fence on my block. As I inhaled the pine scent, I immediately remembered every December from my childhood and the anticipation of Christmas. I had a strong desire to buy one of the trees, for the sake of tradition, but even more for what they evoked: wonder, simplicity, connection to family. The Greek words *nostos* and *algos* translate as "pain" and "return home," respectively, so *nostalgia* is the acute homesickness that's triggered when we're reminded of our past. The bittersweet recognition that a time and a place in our life has passed us by and cannot be reclaimed smacks of the dissatisfaction of impermanence.

While there isn't anything inherently painful about change, we struggle deeply against it. The fight against impermanence sets off low-grade anxiety and tension, a rigid, misplaced hope that if we can find the right combination of things, we'll be able to keep it all together. The truth is that people leave. Attraction fades. Our plump and juicy skin gets wrinkled, no matter how much we spend on retinol cream. You will change along with your interests. So will your lover, and that's okay. The cookies are gone, and I want another. My body will inevitably fail me. When Shunryu Suzuki was asked by a student to reduce Buddhism to a single phrase, he answered point-blank, "Everything changes."[2] It's one of the hardest truths to swallow, and it causes us inexhaustible suffering. As Frida Kahlo captured in her diaries, "Nothing is absolute. Everything changes, everything moves, everything revolutionizes, everything flies away."[3] In the meantime, we just stack sandbags against the tsunami and hope for the best.

The third type of dukkha is the ominous-sounding "all-pervasive dissatisfaction." It's that deep-down chronic dissatisfaction that's like a persistent little itch that we can't quite scratch, even if our lack of accessibility doesn't keep us from trying. Even if nothing is wrong, per se, all-pervasive dissatisfaction leads us to believe that our situation could be a little more interesting, comfortable, or satisfying. We find it in the shifting of our leg or the checking of our email while waiting in line at Trader Joe's. We're quick to add a little salt to heighten flavor or flip the channel to anything else. All-pervasive dissatisfaction is related to the fundamental awkwardness of just being in our own skin; a low-level case of restless everything syndrome. In most cases, we bypass it altogether by giving ourselves a low dose of entertainment or stimulation so we can avoid the discomfort of inhabiting ourselves and occupying blank space. Simply being with this shade of dukkha, without filler or additives, is the fast track to learning to love our own company. In many ways, this stealthy form of dissatisfaction is the nut that gets cracked when we spend time on the meditation cushion.

Your Suffering Is the Least Interesting Thing About You

Let's just all admit that sometimes we have a hard time. If you're finding that the whole suffering bit rings true for you, then let me be (perhaps) the first to tell you that, yes, your experience is valid; you are inherently whole and capable, and there is nothing wrong with you. If you are having a hard time, that's okay. Maybe it feels like you "should" have gotten your life together by now, or you're down on yourself because you haven't been thinking positively enough. (This is a strange catch-22, but I know from experience that it happens.) You're just having the experience of being human. Dukkha is dukkha, and I love you.

In some Buddhist iconography, the pain of suffering is represented as being struck by an arrow. Not very subtle, but it gets its point across. Not getting what we want, experiencing loss, and feeling ill at ease in our own skin are painful. Hence, the arrow. No one wants an arrow in the eye, or any place else for that matter, but we all suffer, and if we haven't developed any sort of relationship with our suffering, we're likely to respond in a way referred to as "shooting a second arrow." We feel discomfort, and then we double down by fighting against it or judging ourselves as wrong because the pain happened in the first place. This is when our demons storm the gate. Whatever your particular demon material is—shame, aggression, fixation, self-doubt—your demons arise not because of dukkha, but in response to dukkha.

While teaching a meditation class or hosting a coaching program, I inevitably encounter folks who tentatively share how off the mark they feel with their progress. "My leg fell asleep . . . and then my mind started wandering. I found the whole meditation really hard." Or, "I feel so far behind in the program. I know people who are way ahead of me, and I just don't think I will ever catch up." Some of these folks will then shoot the second arrow, by judging themselves for their difficult experience:

It's not good enough.

That's a terrible excuse.

I just can't get my shit together.

I feel like I just really suck at this.

First, there's difficulty. Then we beat ourselves up for experiencing it. *Hello, self-aggression. Fancy seeing you here.* I have shot the second arrow a million times or more, and believe me when I say it's not helpful. Some of us can use self-criticism as fuel to do "better," but criticism is a fuel that doesn't burn clean. Self-criticism simply isn't sustainable. Whipping ourselves into submission not only piles discomfort onto discomfort, it also reifies the belief that we should be punished and pushed.

In *Zen Mind, Beginner's Mind*, Shunryu Suzuki shares a story from the Samyuktagama Sutra about four kinds of horses: wise ones, skillful ones, poor ones, and delusional ones. The wise horse, it's said, will run in all directions, at all paces, and at the driver's will without ever needing to see a whip. The skillful horse will run well, but only just before the threat of the whip reaches its skin. The poor horse will run only once it's felt the pain of the whip. And the delusional horse will only run, he concludes, "after the pain penetrates to the marrow of its bones. You can imagine how difficult it is for the fourth one to learn how to run!"[4] All to say, criticizing ourselves is not a great recipe for happiness, certainly not for self-love, and it's not all that effective in the long run. The second arrow is just more dukkha. And don't you have enough already?

When I hear these admissions in class I find it helpful to ask if anyone else can relate. On average, a dozen hands will go up. Foot fell asleep? Look! You are not alone. Feeling desperately behind? It statistically can't be so, because half of the class is also "behind." Normalizing our discomfort can be a healing modality unto itself.

One of the more famous stories from the Buddhist canon of teachings is that of Kisa Gotami and the mustard seed. Kisa Gotami is a bit of a tragic heroine in the traditional tales. In one story, she loses her entire family in one day and wanders the lands mad with grief until she encounters the Buddha and his teachings. In the story of the mustard seed, from the Therigatha, a book of poetry written by and about the first Buddhist nuns, our heroine is wracked with grief at the death of her infant son.[5] Unable to reconcile the fact that he has already passed, she seeks out someone who can give him medicine that will revive him. This part of Kisa Gotami's story, the inability to relate to the reality of impermanence, is painfully relatable to me. The desire to stay in the bargaining stage of grief with the misplaced hope that something, anything, will come along and put the pieces back together.

Kisa Gotami hears of the Buddha, who had been teaching in India, and travels to him with the body of her deceased boy draped in her arms. She throws herself at the Buddha's mercy and pleads for a cure to bring her son back. It's said that the Buddha considers her case for a moment and then promises that he will do as she asks if she collects a single mustard seed from the home of a family that has not experienced loss. Kisa Gotami springs into action, knocking on every door in the village with her singular request. As the story goes, at each door she is confronted with stories of loss. The death of a daughter. A wife. A cousin. A friend. No home in the village could fulfill her request. It is then that Kisa Gotami realized the universality of sorrow, and she returned to the Buddha. The recognition that her grief wasn't isolated in some ways healed her.

As tempting as it can be, in those moments when we're visiting the swampland of the soul, to anchor our identity in our sadness, our struggles, our disputes, the First Noble Truth says, "No. You are not alone." You're in excellent company. Your suffering is valid. You have nothing to hide. And also, your struggles are not the sum total of who you are. This understanding opens the door for us to make dukkha workable, relatable, and, possibly in our quest for healing, a catalyzing force of connection. When we understand that the full spectrum of dukkha is a condition of being human, rather than a character defect, we're freed to feel our pain without taking it so personally. This act of recognizing our humanity can prevent us from shooting ourselves with those second arrows of shame, blame, and isolation.

Let It Break Your Heart

The reality of our lives is that they are fragile. Everything changes, and everything goes, and if we have experienced love in any of its forms, this reality is bound to break our hearts. This First Noble Truth reminds us that connection, in all its joy and beauty, is also a path to suffering. When we love anyone or anything within the backdrop of impermanence, we are bound to have our hearts broken. This is unavoidable. This also doesn't have to be a problem. As much as connection inevitably leads to suffering, suffering can also lead us to connection. As in the story of Kisa Gotami, at some point we realize that we are not alone in this. That realization can be a catalyzing force, leading us to extend a helping hand to our neighbors. In heartbreak there is a tremendous opportunity to be broken open into a more expansive sense of empathy, appreciation, and love. This beautiful line of poetry from Naomi Shihab Nye reminds us that when we demonize our suffering, it never has the chance to show us its profound wisdom, which is tenderness, empathy, and kindness: "Before you know kindness as the deepest thing inside, you must know sorrow as the other deepest thing."[6]

This opportunity of empathy and connection that exists in the universality of heartbreak is grounds for developing the heart of a Buddha, or Bodhicitta, which translates as "awakened heart-mind." Our hearts awaken to one another when we feel the shared challenge of being a human on this planet. An awakened heart-mind is where our deep and abiding courage springs from—the courage to face our own demons directly, as well as to be helpful when we witness the suffering of others. Chögyam Trungpa refers to this openhearted quality as our genuine heart of sadness, and he goes on to remind us that "real fearlessness is the product of tenderness. It comes from letting the world tickle your heart, your raw and beautiful heart."[7] Rather than resisting or unleashing our demons, we can feel them storming the gates in the moments when dukkha makes itself apparent. *Hello, shame, resentment, indignation, fear. Thank you for the information.* When we recognize that the value of our painful moments is that they serve as a gateway to our own tender hearts, we can begin widening that field of tenderness to include even our most difficult emotions. Kindness and compassion neutralize our demon material. The world is going to break your heart. First Noble Truth. We get to decide if it breaks us open into empathy or into sharp little pieces.

On the Spot Practice The next time you catch yourself prodded by a demon while deep in the rabbit hole of your suffering, pause. Let the story you are telling yourself go, and come back into your body. Place your hand on your heart. Take a breath. Let your body relax, even just a little bit. See if you can connect with the tenderness of your Bodhicitta, your awakened heart.

Welcome to the Charnel Grounds

The Second Noble Truth

> Try to exclude the possibility of suffering which the
> order of nature and the existence of free wills involve,
> and you find that you have excluded life itself.
>
> C. S. Lewis, *The Problem of Pain*

A number of years ago I spent a week in solitary meditation in the Berkshire Mountains. The first day of practice was easeful, and I relished the silence and space created by being off the grid with no email or responsibilities. I went to sleep early and woke up deeply refreshed the next morning; my life was simplified down to the essentials of meditation, three meals, and rest. It was divine. Until day two. Then I promptly began to split apart at the seams. First, my body caught on fire. Everything hurt in sitting meditation, and there was absolutely no way to get comfortable. My hips and legs felt tight and rusty. My lower back and shoulders were searing. Every part of my body was fussy. Then came my cravings. I wanted sugar, and chocolate, and sex, and a glass of wine, and basically anything that I could put in my mouth that would take the edge off all of the space, all of the silence, and all of the being with me. There was nothing happening. Just practice. But in that moment, I was seriously considering hitchhiking home so I could have the experience of doing anything else besides being with my mind and my body. This was a gnarly case of restless everything syndrome, heightened by the fact that I couldn't distract myself or tamp it down with a glass of malbec. I'm not proud to say that on that day I ransacked the cupboards of my cabin and emptied into my mouth the single stale pack of Domino sugar I found, scraping the remaining crystals from the inside with my pinkie. To date, this was the most vivid experience of the Second Noble Truth—the causes of dissatisfaction—that I've had.

It's here that the Second Noble Truth follows up on the First Noble Truth to say that if we experience dissatisfaction in a number of forms through our lifetime, there is a reason why. And it isn't, contrary to popular belief, because we are a total screwup. Or because our world is on fire, thanks to a bunch of ignorant jerks. From a Buddhist perspective, our dissatisfaction is established in three primary qualities: fixating on what we want, resisting what we don't want, and having no idea that this internal tug-of-war is happening all day, every day, ad infinitum. The cause of suffering can be boiled down to Three Root Poisons: attachment, aggression, and ignorance. Or, in their more inflamed manifestations, greed, hate, and delusion. *Hello, demon material.*

Attachment: The First Root Poison

It's so distinctly human to want and want and want. Other animals, of course, want as well. Food, shelter, partnership, community. Desire isn't unique to us as a species. But we do have these wonderfully creative human minds that are able to invent new things to want and to then collect them, which, of course, we do. There are specific neighborhoods in Brooklyn that I find it hard, painful even, to walk through because the perfectly curated display windows in the impossibly aspirational boutiques have me nearly pressing my body against the glass, begging the employees to take my money. "I had no idea that this hand-dyed Moroccan virgin lambs' wool blanket existed, and now I can't *fathom* existing without it!" Our creativity and imagination can make desire feel boundless. If we can dream it up or stumble upon it we can urgently aspire to have it. Most of us are pretty insatiable that way.

We also have a very strange relationship with pleasure. We routinely cheat ourselves of perfectly subtle moments of pleasure because of our inability to be present for them. The invigorating crispness of the air on our walk to work or the beauty of the shifting morning light is often lost on us as we ruminate on something or move through the world on total autopilot until we reach our destination. In my case, I'd be too busy fantasizing about how I could afford that ridiculous and gorgeous blanket to feel the satisfactory crunch of dried leaves beneath my feet. We can become so desensitized to beauty and pleasure that they rarely even register unless they're in mass quantity form and orgasmically thrilling. No wonder we're so fixated on more. The catch is that it's in the pursuit of more that we deny ourselves so much. A mindfulness practice can be exceedingly helpful in reorienting our sensitivities to the tiniest pleasures of our lives. More on that later.

As a child I remember watching the 1971 version of *Willy Wonka & the Chocolate Factory* and having the distinct sense that I should be identifying with Charlie, the humble and good-hearted protagonist. But I didn't. He was flavorless. I loved Veruca Salt. I would twirl around and sing along excitedly each time the bratty antagonist broke into her encore song,

"I want the whole world . . . Give it to me now!"[1] I can see now that part of her appeal was that she was a young female modeling how to be vocal about and unashamed of her desires. She wasn't apologetic, nice, and well-mannered the way that girls my age were taught to be. She knew what she wanted and demanded that she get it. Of course, in retrospect I recognize that entitlement and self-worth have a very different bedrock, even if they sometimes present similarly.

In many ways Veruca Salt is the ideal avatar for this first root poison of wanting—better, more, and now. In Pali, the ancient language of the Buddha, this sense of wanting translates as "fixation," "craving," "grasping," or "thirst." What the Buddha was referring to is the natural orientation that we have to appreciate what is lovely. As Ralph Waldo Emerson pointed out, "Beauty is the form under which the intellect prefers to study the world."[2] Where our delusion or demon material kicks up, however, is in that split second in which our appreciation of beauty gets rigid and possessive. *Hello, fixation, grasping, and greed. You thirsty little demons.* There is the fundamental confusion that either we are not enough or our experience is not enough, and so we latch on to people, objects, and aspirations with the belief that they will make us happy. From this perspective, not only is suffering the equalizer of all living beings, so is our desire for happiness. We're pretty simple that way.

On some level, we mistakenly believe that happiness lives in the things that we want and the experiences that we're aspiring to have. Even if this belief isn't explicit, it's revealed in how doggedly we will work for our long-term desires, and also how frequently we reach for the more instantly attainable pleasures. Think about it. When was the last time that you wandered to the kitchen and stared blankly through an open refrigerator because you wanted something? Or scrolled through Instagram, emails, or online shopping sites while sitting in a waiting room? It's so habitual for us to move toward what is pleasurable, or at the very least distract ourselves from what is not pleasurable, that this behavior is essentially wired into our factory settings. Eat the yummy thing. Look at the yummy photos. Cuddle with the yummy person. These are the G-rated versions, of course.

If we're honest, on some level happiness does appear to be in the "thing." Happiness could legitimately be a brussels sprout pizza and a bottle of red wine on a Friday night with my friends. Perhaps not everlasting-bliss levels of happiness, but certainly a dose of momentary satisfaction. Neuroscience has verified that we receive a powerful hit of feel-good chemicals when we get the thing that we want to have or have an experience that we seek. Public recognition hits us with a jolt of serotonin. Dopamine fires when we hit a goal or eat a cupcake. Oxytocin floods our body when we spend time with friends or receive a hug, a kiss, or a cuddle.[3] This is a beautiful thing, and I for one wouldn't trade this chemical cocktail of feel-good sensations for anything. Isn't it marvelous that as humans we have not just one but multiple nuanced ways of receiving powerful hits of pleasure? Yes. Please. More. Please.

However, "more, please" is where this pursuit of pleasure gets a bit twisted. Because pleasure obviously feels good, and feeling good makes us happy, we do the simple math and make the unexamined assumption that pleasure equals happiness. It's an easy assumption to make. But one which is fundamentally flawed, the Buddha taught, because pleasure was designed to fade. Once the cupcake is eaten and we've brushed our teeth, or the cuddle session has ended—either for the evening, or permanently—all of these yummy feel-good chemicals stop flowing, which keeps us on the treadmill of wanting. Wanting more. Wanting now. Enjoying pleasure for pleasure's sake is delightful. Happiness that's contingent on pleasure, however, is unsustainable. It's also, frankly, exhausting, and to some extent extremely limiting. We can easily find ourselves feeling tight, dissatisfied, or emotionally unraveled when our narrow preconditions for happiness aren't met.

Of course, this doesn't mean that we should aspire to some cardboard existence devoid of pleasure, desire, and ambition. That sounds, frankly, tragic. However, it does mean that it might be in our best interest to keep our finger on the pulse of just how much our clinging to "only the good stuff, please," runs the show in our lives, particularly when it comes to our approval rating of ourselves. Is there anything that we're trying to outrun by chasing after the dream? Is what we want an effort to prove ourselves to be lovable or worthy?

Sometime around 2012, in a public talk at The Interdependence Project with the Venerable Robina Courtin,[4] one audience member asked her a question about how to reconcile the trouble with attachment and this natural human desire. Surely, it can't be a bad thing, right? We would all be a pile of ambitionless mashed potatoes if we didn't have some amount of drive and desire, she reasoned. Ven. Robina answered emphatically, "Of course!" Her response was this: "It's okay to ask what you want; don't be scared of knowing what you want. But the test is when [you] don't get it . . . that's the practice." Or—and here's the kicker—you get exactly what you want, and it doesn't make you as happy as you imagined.

Aggression: The Second Root Poison

Back in India, circa 500 BC, the Buddha would send his disciples to practice meditation in the most challenging places possible, such as charnel grounds. Charnel grounds were like cemeteries, except the bodies were not buried; they were left to decompose in the sun while scavengers picked them apart, making these places particularly gruesome. When the Buddhist teacher Pema Chödrön was asked what a modern-day comparison to charnel grounds might be, she cited the emergency room of a hospital, where something visceral and raw about the human condition can be witnessed. As a metaphor, charnel grounds can be seen as any environment steeped in this demon material that we all work with, personally and culturally. The demons of fear, depression, jealousy, and intolerance are all markers of a charnel environment.

I'd argue that social media is a modern charnel ground. Holding your seat when faced with the inevitably more fabulous lives of others is an advanced practice of maintaining a sense of self-worth. It's reminiscent of the Buddha facing Mara on the eve of his awakening. Except swap out his demon horde with a gaggle of #fitspo models smiling brightly in swan-shaped inner tubes. Try touching unshakable confidence when your contribution to digital society is being rated each step of the way. For many of us, it's nearly impossible to develop a private, self-held opinion of ourselves that is independent of the digital feedback loop. I've seen grown women both inflate with confidence and be reduced to dust with the click of an Instagram comment. Comparison breeds self-aggression and, in the same vein as the traditional charnel grounds, nothing gets buried on the internet, just aggressively picked apart.

The second root poison that the Buddha spoke of is the poison of aggression, ill will, and aversion. Unlike attachment, it's much easier for many of us to spot this poison because it doesn't feel good. Weaponizing social media, or any media, as ammo to use against ourselves feels terrible. Alternatively, aggression might be triggered when our back starts to hurt in meditation or we're placed in a stressful situation. In its muted form, this poison manifests as subtle annoyance or irritation, the feeling that arises when a gnat is circulating inches from our face. In its full-blown expression, this poison manifests as repulsion and hatred. The interplay between the root poisons is symbiotic: for example, the moment we see a gnat circulating, our desire to be unbothered is disrupted and we feel annoyance, wanting to clap it out of existence between our palms. For the sake of seeing both attachment and aggression clearly, we'll be teasing them out separately; however, they very frequently walk hand in hand.

Our path can become particularly painful when we direct aggression toward ourselves, either for not living up to our own standards or for feeling a general sense of unhappiness with ourselves. When I first began meditating in earnest in my twenties, one of the quickest and clearest revelations that snapped into focus was just how nasty I was to myself. It was as if there was a tiny and unforgiving woman living in a very tidy, austere part of my mind who watched every single move I made and spliced in her own critiques. It was, as you can imagine, a horrifying revelation. I had a general sense of how hard I was on myself; we all have some basic self-awareness. However, it wasn't until I began sitting in meditation with a front-row view of my mind that I realized how frequently a news ticker of hostile content passed across my screen. I felt like I had been living with a bully and had developed a case of Stockholm syndrome. I had just accepted those critiques as the truth.

I began referring to this voice as my inner Miranda Priestly, affectionately named after the fashion force and editrix in the film *The Devil Wears Prada*. It's easy to slap unflattering labels on women for displaying qualities we would applaud in the opposite sex, so I want to say that I empathize with women in power. However, my internalized Miranda Priestly, fiercely lodged in my cerebral cortex, was the spitting image of only the critical bits of the stereotypical powerful woman: uncompromising, demanding, perfectionistic, and impossible to please. After becoming aware of her very existence, I heard her yammering from behind her blunt bob and sunglasses all the time. "She's looking at your pimples. You can see your fat rolls in that dress. They're laughing politely because you're not funny. When you open your mouth, they'll see how dumb you are. When you take off your shirt, he'll see how gross you are. Blah blah blah blah blah . . ."

To some extent, we all have an inner editor—a voice that is critical, spiteful, and unkind. If fixation, grasping, and greed are the demon qualities of attachment, then comparison, judgment, and annoyance are the demon qualities of aggression—the gnarlier aspects of ourselves that spring forth when our attachment doesn't get what it wants.

Comparative suffering is a social phenomenon that refers to our tendency to look around at everyone else to see how we measure up. What standard should I be aiming for here? What do the people around me do for work? How much money do they make? What do they have? We may not even consciously realize that we are doing this. As social creatures we have a natural impulse to gauge whether we have enough by looking into the bowl of the person next to us. We understand our place in the pecking order this way. This impulse is related to our biological need for safety, love, and belonging. In the not-too-distant past, if we lived exclusively in a rural town, this might have meant looking into the bowls of a few dozen people, or a few thousand maximum if we dwelled in a city. When it comes to this impulse in our modern world, the biggest difference, of course, is the internet. The internet can be a glorious tool of connection, outreach, and activation. By hosting online classes and talks, I've met folks from around the globe whom I would never have connected with were my work relegated to my city alone. My heart expands three sizes each time I launch a meditation series into the digital ether and the signal is returned by a real human being who has invited me into their home to practice and then reaches out to me as a result. This is the wisdom side of our expanded network; it's a mirror of our interdependence.

In its neurotic form, our global village now gives us unlimited bowls to look into and compare ours to. We have infinite opportunities to judge our worth based on millions of other people: what they are doing, wearing, eating, and making; who they're dating; and how good they do or don't look doing these things. Unless we have a workable relationship with our inner critic, this can be the perfect recipe for self-doubt to pull us underground.

The Eight Worldly Winds: Investing Our Sense of Self in Unstable Markets

The Eight Worldly Winds is a set of teachings that showcase where craving and aversion blow us back and forth. They're traditionally considered four sets of forces, or our four most powerful worldly concerns: we want to pursue one and fear the other. The pursuit of status and the fear of disgrace. The pursuit of gain and the fear of loss. The pursuit of praise and the fear of blame. The pursuit of pleasure and the fear of pain. Essentially, they refer to what we fixate on cultivating and what we try to avoid at all costs. One way to think about these winds is that they are the primary energies behind the cycle of self-doubt. When we don't have faith in our fundamental worth, we trade and collect these currencies instead as vouchers of our value. The trouble is that they are fickle, flimsy markets that we have very little control of. When they're on the up, we feel amazing. However, when they fail us, our sense of self is what takes the hit.

THE CURRENCY OF STATUS AND THE BANKRUPTCY OF DISGRACE

Who would you be without your reputation?

The first time that I saw the Venerable Robina Courtin give a public talk, she leaned in close to the audience, paused, and candidly observed, "One of our worst attachments, Buddha says, is to what other people think of us. And often that runs everything we do, and it's like a fucking nightmare."[5] It was as though she had just seen into me, plucked out my deepest neurosis, and dangled it in front of my face where I could finally see it. I took my refuge vows, the vows one takes to officially become a Buddhist, with her a year later. Status is one of the Eight Worldly Winds that "the world spins after," as the Buddha put it. Anyone who has ever been shunned from eating at a particular cafeteria table or has had their reputation smeared learns this. Whether it's the role that we play in our social circle, the position we hold in our community's hierarchy, or the number of Instagram followers we have, it's so easy to invest our sense of self-worth in the answer to this question: What do people think of me?

Whether explicitly or subtly, we tend to believe that our value is reflected in the collective opinion of others. We're taught early on to invest our worth in the way that we're perceived. The idea of not being liked is unbearable. The worldly wind of status, or fame, popularity, and reputation, hits at our desire for approval and our deep, tribal longing to belong. At the end of the day, we are social creatures, pack animals in pretty clothes really, and our fixation on achieving good standing among our peers can run so deep that it's nearly imperceptible.

The Buddha taught that status, like all winds, is bound to blow in the other direction. No matter how hard we try to prevent it, people's tastes change, and interest in what we have to offer is fickle. We may make an unpopular choice or a bad decision and lose the favor of our peers. Some people just won't like us. If we're ruled by status, this is a hard realization that we might find completely untenable. Back in 2014, the Dalai Lama was visiting New York and hosting a weekend of teachings for the public. As I crossed the street to the theater that was hosting him for the weekend, I was submerged in the sound of hundreds of protesters whose rally cry was "Fake Dalai Lama! The Dalai Lama is a liar!" They gathered outside the venue all weekend, holding signs, chanting insults, denouncing his legitimacy as a teacher. I was gobsmacked. The Dalai Lama has haters? The man lives his life to promote peace and compassion! If there are people who don't like the Dalai Lama, I reason, then I should give up on the idea of achieving a perfect status report, and maybe so should you. Negotiating the way that we're perceived by others is an endless, impossible task.

If our sense of worth is based on the approval of others, we'll always be haunted by the question of what people will think of us. It will seep into our decision-making process, subtly ruling our world. We may even choose to not rock the boat or to not stand up for what's right because doing so is unpopular, and the threat of being an outcast slices our self-worth to the bone. Of course, there's no guarantee, ever, that choosing what is popular will keep you safe or that choosing what is right will make you heard. This is the fickle nature of the Eight Worldly Winds. Investing our self-worth in our reputation is like buying stocks in an unstable market. Disgrace—or perhaps worse, irrelevance—are just a strong gust of wind away.

THE CURRENCY OF GAIN AND THE BANKRUPTCY OF LOSS

Who would you be if you lost all that you have?

The popular myth of limitless gain is embedded so deeply in our cultural psyche that it can be easy to miss. However, if we look, we can see it everywhere—in the Home Depot slogan "always improving" and in the American economic model that hinges on exponential growth. It's in the advice to "always stay hungry." To that, I say, excuse me. I don't want to stay hungry. I want to have enough to eat and then go take a satisfied nap in the corner, thank you very much. There is this idea that we can always be increasing, gaining, getting better, collecting more, and if we lose, we feel personally diminished.

This mythology is also embedded in our language. Winners *win*. Losers *lose*. Failures *fail*. A meditation student of mine was floored by the revelation that she had identified so strongly with the predicament of being "broke" financially that she considered herself to be "broken," as in damaged and needing repair. As overidentifying with our confusion supports our confusion, the English language supports our internalization of certain messages as well, such as that of endless gains. However, the idea of always improving flies directly in the face of the laws of nature. What grows and gains exponentially in the kingdoms of animals and plants? Nothing. There is a growing season and a fallow season, which is by design. Gain and loss go hand in hand. Unchecked growth of an organism destroys the ecosystem that it inhabits. It becomes a cancer to its host. Gain and growth without loss and decay are simply unsustainable. This is a natural system of checks and balances.

So why do we fear loss so deeply? Well, for one, it's exceedingly painful. If you've ever experienced loss, which I wager you have (*hello, First Noble Truth*), then you know that I'm stating the obvious. Because our nature is to hold very tightly to what we love, admire, and need, losing what we're holding on to can be extraordinarily traumatic. What we hold on to and what we've lost can even come to define our very sense of self. I have a dear friend whose father recently retired. As a company man, he found his sense of self in his work, in his allegiance to his employer, in that traditional "up the corporate ladder" kind of way. After forty years of dedicated service, her father was given a nice watch and a retirement party and was sent off to enjoy his golden years. My friend has described the loss of identity he's faced as heartbreaking to witness. He seems stuck with this question: If I am without this work, this community, this title, who in the world am I? Of course there is nothing unique about this situation; we build a refuge in our work and in our communities. There is nothing fundamentally wrong with this. However, if our self-worth hinges on always gaining, acquiring, and getting "better," we can easily feel debased and without purpose or value when we experience loss.

It's worth acknowledging that there is also very little tolerance for loss in a society that heralds unlimited growth and gain. This, incidentally, can make us feel very isolated when we do lose something, or someone. Loss can be tremendously lonely. It can also lead to crushing expectations that we should always be getting "better" or summon a paralyzing fear of failure that prevents us from even leaving the starting gate. Loss is naturally painful. The blame, fear, and stigmatization of loss that are then placed on our experience is the heartbreaking second arrow. Demon material, amplified.

Who would you be if you weren't right?

One of my distinct specialties is the ability to hold on to crit-icism for decades. I can clearly recall my mother telling me point-blank that I was a terrible storyteller. I was seven, sitting in the backseat of her red Ford Fiesta. I even remember what I was wearing. In her defense, I had a penchant for rewinding halfway through a story to include missing details for context. I still do this, and I'll be darned if I didn't hold on to that inter-nalized feedback for years. I can also recall my junior-high crush calling me chubby, my beloved acting professor insinuating that my makeup looked like rosacea, and my husband referencing me in a public talk, asking, "Couldn't she just get up and do the dishes after dinner for once?" To his credit, I'm certain it was kinder than the version that I'm prone to remembering. Have I mentioned that I can also be petty? Trust that if you insulted my outfit in 1998, your name is on a list somewhere.

Objectively, all of the affronts I mentioned bear some kernel of truth. I can count on one hand the number of times I've done my dishes right after dinner, and I was heavy-handed with the blush brush in my twenties. However, truth doesn't necessarily make criticism any more palatable, particularly if the criticism hits on one of our insecurities. Beyond that, I love being right. I'm essentially addicted to hearing my name with only nice words attached and cannot stand to be spoken of otherwise. I don't want my imperfections revealed; I only want my strengths displayed. This, of course, is not at all unique. It's the nature of the worldly wind of praise and blame. We fortify ourselves with the assurances and compliments of others and avoid critique.

However, if our sense of worth is built upon hearing our name with only nice things attached, not only will one well-timed rejection from the right person carry the power to tear us down entirely, but we may also be willfully deaf to constructive criticism that might be useful. There's very little room for looking at our blind spots when doing so threatens our entire sense of self. Sometimes we are genuinely wrong, or at the very least misinformed and misguided, and admitting this to ourselves and others can be the key to relinquishing harmful behaviors. In her essay "On Self-Respect," Joan Didion asserts that "people with self-respect have the courage of their mistakes. They know the price of things."[6] Yes, but how many of us have the courage to face our shortcomings all the time?

Ironically, those of us who are the most intolerant to criticism are generally the quickest to dole it out. It is the fault of society, the fault of our lover, the fault of anyone but ourselves, because that would be too devastating to bear. But taking refuge in our innocence leads to a certain fragility. Being "right" is currency that doesn't divest and requires constant reinvestment. We're always on the lookout for threats to our righteousness, on guard against the slightest critique. Investing our sense of self in praise and correctness is a trap of ceaseless maintenance and anxiety. There can be no rest when our guard is always up.

THE CURRENCY OF PLEASURE AND THE BANKRUPTCY OF PAIN
Who do you become in the face of discomfort?

When I first began dating my now husband, he asked me what I regarded as one of the most romantic questions I'd ever been asked: "Are you willing to meet me in discomfort?" For me, the romance of this question is that it cracked through some of the idealization that we tend to do early in the dating stages. He didn't ask me if I'd be willing to go on a nonstop pleasure cruise on which both of us would be on our best behavior, playing out each other's adolescent fantasies of love. He asked if I would shovel the mud with him. His was an invitation to experience it all.

For the most part, being human involves continually looking for that pleasure cruise and making our very best effort to take up permanent residence on that ship. As it was with Siddhartha in the palace, there's nothing necessarily wrong with taking refuge in pleasure. I've taken refuge in ice cream plenty of times. Until I've eaten a bit too much of it and start to feel queasy and bloated. Of course, herein lies the rub: the refuge of pleasure is not sturdy or lasting, so it keeps us nomadic and hunting for more.

Pleasure and pain serve as the master undercurrent that raises the other worldly winds: Status is pleasurable, disgrace is painful. Same with gain and loss, praise and blame. These pairings are just the root poisons riding the winds of delusion, taking different shapes with the promise that this time, this time, it will finally click into place and stay there. In the Buddhist text Lokavipatti Sutta, one of the Buddha's teachings is translated as "these conditions among human beings are inconstant, impermanent, subject to change. Knowing this, the wise person, mindful, ponders these changing conditions. Desirable things don't charm the mind, undesirable ones bring no resistance."[7] Essentially, if we learn to rest in discomfort and enjoy pleasure for what it is—a fleeting, wispy thing—without getting overwhelmed by either, we cease to be blown around. In order to journey back to feeling our infallible value, it's necessary to understand the obstacles to our self-worth, such as the demon material we're working with and the currencies we deal in. On the Earth and in the soil, everything is workable because it's of the Earth, and so it all belongs. All experiences are just fodder, material, sometimes compost. All we need to do is roll up our sleeves.

Ignorance: The Third Root Poison

What fundamentally underlies the whole structure of attachment and aggression is that we don't have faith in our basic goodness, and so we identify with these transient states. We are fundamentally ignorant of our wakefulness and create out of this third root poison all sorts of stories about ourselves so as to prop up the ego. We hold on to our education, our social groups, our beliefs, and the roles that we play as though these are concretely "us." Even seemingly solid identity markers like gender are being both questioned and dismantled at this time, realized as more fluid contracts than we thought. We cannot hold on to them any more than the ego markers of our job or relationship status.

In Greek and Roman theater, actors wore masks called *personas*, which is the root word for *personality*, so the audience would know the different characters they were playing. Not so differently in our own lives, we have different personas for different situations. There is the "me" who shows up at work and makes watercooler banter. People there know me a certain way. When I go out with my friends, I might have a looser or more uninhibited, less buttoned-down persona. I have a persona who shows up to family functions. Often family dynamics have shaped this one. "Jennifer brought the drama this year—that is such a Jennifer thing to do . . ."

Donning different personas is not a problem in our day-to-day life; we often need to play different roles in different situations in order to relate to them skillfully. How I show up in sessions with my clients is different from how I show up on Friday night with my friends. Highlighting different aspects of ourselves in the context of the environment can be a way of creating healthy boundaries and practicing skillful means. Problems arise when we are ignorant to the extent that we forget that we are an ever-shifting being who is participating in the world fluidly and thus begin to self-identify with a particular role. The teacher Jetsunma Tenzin Palmo has compared this case of mistaken identity to an actor who continues to play the role of Hamlet even after he's left the stage. He's forgotten that he's not actually Hamlet. We become ignorant of who we truly are, our own wakefulness, and get addicted to playing up who we want to be or are expected to be.

One way that ignorance can manifest as a stuck sense of *ego* is through our self-centeredness, our fear, our arrogance—basically any wiggly demon bits that, in spiritual circles, we are told we need to transcend in order to be free. While these unsavory bits are a part of us, they are not the sum total of who we are by any stretch. Who we are is basically good. Ignorance is the poison that distracts us from that fact and labels those parts of us "wrong."

One heartbreaking thing about working so hard to transcend aspects of ourselves (Who is doing the work anyway? *Ahem.* Ego is.) is that we never really give those bits of ourselves much of a chance to be witnessed as anything other than "bad." They get shoved under the covers, smothered by shame, and grow into starving, shadowy beasts. Maybe they get bypassed for a time, but trust me, our demon qualities do not just transcend. If our demons are any aspect of ourselves that we're prone to demonizing, starving them by ignoring them has the opposite effect. So . . . rather than an internal ego cage fight, what do we do about these bits of "self" that keep us feeling separate, selfish, and scared? Maybe they just need a little attention. A bit of tenderness. A sense of humor when they arise. Pass the scones, won't you? You beautiful nasty beast.

Which demon needs to come to tea, right now? See which one of the root poisons is lodged in your system. The best antidote to our attachment, aggression, ignorance—or any manifestation of these poisons—is to look directly at it. Acknowledge the way this demon material is showing up for you right now. Don't get wrapped up in stories about how to "fix" the way that you feel; just look directly at the way it manifests in your mind through thoughts and feel into the accompanying emotions. Take the time you need to investigate this demon material from a place of humor and levity, if possible. Gently inquire into the nature of your suffering and see if you can remain embodied by gently staying with the breath. This, too, shall pass. Afterward, do something that feels nourishing for yourself, be it taking a long shower, having a cup of tea, or walking the dog.

8

Pure Potential and the Cessation of Suffering

The Third Noble Truth

> If you're going to be a grown-up—which I would define as
> being completely at home in your world no matter how
> difficult the situation—it's because you will allow something
> that's already in you to be nurtured. You allow it to
> grow, you allow it to come out, instead of all the time
> shielding it and protecting it and keeping it buried.
>
> Pema Chödrön, *Start Where You Are*

Like any good guide through the trenches of the psyche, the Buddha knew that he couldn't just introduce us to the shadowlands without also bringing us out the other side. So far, the teachings of the Four Noble Truths have presented us with an analysis of suffering. The First Noble Truth suggests that our discontent is pervasive. Dissatisfaction is felt through the physical pains of having a body, through the heartbreak of impermanence, right down to the subtle aftertaste of boredom when nothing is particularly wrong, but we sense that we could be doing more, or that our experience could be a little bit better. Then, the Second Noble Truth turns on a lightbulb. It highlights that there is a reason why we're discontented in both negligible and heart-crushing ways. The binary of aggression and attachment gives us very little rest. We're continually trying to rearrange our experience to have the exact experience that we want to be having. We protect ourselves against vulnerability, awkwardness, and discomfort. We negotiate the way that we're perceived by others, ad infinitum. We throw our backs into the expectation that we'll be able to get things the way that we want them without ever stopping to first accept the way that they are. To add to this dumpster fire, we generally have no idea that (A) we're participating in this cycle, or that (B) we have intrinsic worth that cannot be added to or subtracted from (ignorance), so we slather ourselves in shame and self-reproach (aggression) while reaching for ever new ways of becoming "better" (attachment). Sound familiar? This starts the whole cycle of suffering all over again and keeps us chasing after the ace of spades (happiness/fulfillment) while shuffling our deck of desires. Frankly, it's exhausting.

If the Buddha's teachings stopped here, it could be devastating. The first two Noble Truths as a stand-alone teaching is a perfect recipe for nihilism, cynicism, and despair, which is why we keep moving toward reconciliation and ultimately finding an alternate approach. This leads us to the Third Noble Truth, which is the news of pure potential: if there are causes of dissatisfaction, then there are also ways to work them out. Every poison has an antidote. We just need to know where to find it. Traditionally, the Third Noble Truth is translated as the "cessation of suffering" and is characterized by letting go and releasing. We might even think of it as loosening our grip a little bit or blurring the lines of the binary. The Third Noble Truth introduces us to the possibility of healing altogether the cycle that this binary binds us to.

Staying Right Sized

The First Noble Truth reminds us that there is a shared humanity in our experience of dukkha, and recognizing this can open our hearts in a powerful way. The writer and cultural critic James Baldwin once reflected, "It was Dostoevsky and Dickens who taught me that the things that tormented me most were the very things that connected me with all the people who were alive, or who ever had been alive. Only if we face these open wounds in ourselves can we understand them in other people."[1] When this truth of our shared humanity is coupled with the realization of our intrinsic worth, we come to recognize a powerful antidote for the Three Root Poisons: We are all deeply significant, and not at all special. We are all profoundly valuable, whole, complete, and sufficient, and there is nothing unique about this. This distinction can bring us back down to earth and to a sense of steady humility that doesn't diminish our worth.

Incidentally, when the Buddha is asked for ways to cultivate well-being in the Maha-mangala Sutta, he names humility as a powerful form of protection for our minds. The sutta goes on to say "a mind that, when touched by the ways of the world, is unshaken, sorrow-less, dustless, at rest."[2] As we explored in the section "Eight Worldly Winds," there's a restlessness that comes with investing our worth in the instability of reputation, praise, gain, and pleasure. The winds of circumstance knock us around so that our sense of self is always in flux. We puff up and expand with what feels like confidence when circumstances are in our favor, but then deflate into self-doubt when they are not. In *Alice's Adventures in Wonderland*, when Alice happens upon a hookah-smoking caterpillar who asks her numerous times who she is, Alice fumbles around in bewilderment looking for an answer, until she admits to the caterpillar, and to herself, "I can't explain *myself*, I'm afraid, Sir . . . because I'm not myself, you see. . . . I'm afraid I can't put it more clearly, . . . for I can't understand it myself to begin with; and being so many different sizes in a day is very confusing."[3] Hear, hear, sister. Truer words have never been spoken. Puffing up with false confidence and deflating with self-doubt can make us feel like we're many different sizes throughout the day, never truly able to occupy space in a way that feels consistent or steady. While humility often gets a bad rap as being ingratiating, lowly, and having a poor opinion of oneself, its roots in the Latin *humus* offer a different perspective, one that's based in the soil, of the Earth, grounded, steady, and fertile. Earth is quietly confident that it is enough, whole unto itself.

Humility can be difficult to remember in a culture of acquisition, where the gospel of "more" is consistently encouraged. This relentless message has two faces: the binary of abundance versus lack. I can testify that the promise of abundance becomes the most appealing when I'm feeling the most internally poverty stricken, fixated on what I want that I don't have. *Hello, demon territory.* As of March 2018, it is estimated that Americans spend upward of 38 billion dollars annually on 2.3 billion square feet of self-storage space to absorb all the excess that no longer fits into our homes.[4] Imagine an area the size of the Hoover Dam filled with our extra electronics, knickknacks, and sporting goods twenty-six times over, or the island of Manhattan four times over. We've created a metropolis of surplus stuff—abundance mentality on overdrive. In contrast, while we're busy building homes for our acquisitions, it's estimated that 554,000 people in America were experiencing homelessness as of 2017.[5] I did a quick bit of math, and for every person in America without adequate shelter, we have 4,000 square feet of storage. This essentially works out to the size of a twelve-room Brooklyn brownstone apartment worth of space per person that's filled with our extra possessions. Excess versus inadequacy. Abundance versus lack. These are the sharp edges of the binary split down the middle of attachment and aggression. Where one side exists in its extreme, so will its shadow in equal depth.

While there's obviously nothing wrong with wanting stuff, having stuff, and storing stuff, these desires present a challenge for staying right sized. The antidote for scarcity isn't excess; the antidote is first defining *enough* and then feeling our way toward it. Learning to rest with what is ample, sufficient, and whole may not be nearly as sexy as abundance, but it is a place where we can learn to rest. Staying right sized is about stepping out of the binary. There is sturdiness in enoughness, like the sturdiness of the Earth itself. When we can step outside of the binary of abundance versus lack, we're given a much more stable base to work from, and one that is just the right size.

Feeding the Hungry Ghosts

Every July in Japan there is ceremony called *segaki*, which roughly translates as "feeding the hungry ghosts." It's an annual practice with the express purpose of doing what the name suggests. Hungry ghosts are called forth from the shadowlands and given an offering to sate them. In Buddhist iconography, these hungry ghosts aren't the bedsheet-wearing, house-haunting Casper types that might come to mind when you think of ghosts. They're more akin to lost souls, outcast creatures wracked by the specific pain of persistent, unquenchable longing. I associate these creatures with Gollum from *The Lord of the Rings* trilogy. He's frightening at first glance, and I wouldn't want to encounter him in a dark cave. But there's also something sympathetic about his wasted, painful fixation on the ring that makes me root for his redemption.

In a similar fashion, hungry ghosts are both terrifying and sad. Some of these *gaki* or *preta,* as they are called in Sanskrit, are depicted in paintings and writing with long, thin necks, tiny pinholes for mouths, and the protruding ribs and distended bellies characteristic of chronic malnourishment. Others are said to roam looking desperately for food and water, only to have them turn to fire in their mouths when they consume them. They are unable to get their needs met or to grasp the object of their desire, no matter how hard they try. The *jikininki* are hungry ghosts bound by repulsive cravings, a gaping hunger for things like rotting corpses and human feces. The tragedy of the jikininki is that they are self-aware enough to be overcome by shame and self-loathing when they give in to what they want. They find themselves repulsive. And yet they cannot shake the compulsive craving that keeps them locked in a cycle of shame. Others of these hungry ghosts have simply been forgotten. With no ancestors or loved ones to make offerings to their memories, they wander through the wastelands starving. Sometimes, if the circumstances are right, they are able to find their salvation through the kindness of the living.

Hungry ghosts are personifications of our own states of fixation and despair, which is perhaps what makes their iconography so potent. The First and Second Noble Truths remind us that we've all experienced at least one of these stricken states of mind, when we've been desperate for some fulfillment that doesn't quite do the trick. As we explore the cessation of our own fixations, or the Third Noble Truth, it can be helpful to offer our own demons the space to be seen, coupled with the gifts of our affection. We can do this any time we notice our own afflicted states of mind, or more formally in meditation, by turning our attention explicitly toward the source of our affliction. The following meditation practice is one method for feeding your hungry ghosts.

MEDITATION PRACTICE
Make Space for Your Demons

- As with the mindfulness of breath meditation, begin by finding a comfortable seat. Again, there are no rules, as long as your body is upright and in a position that feels sustainable. Take a few minutes to bookend your practice by feeling your body in space, sensing your environment, and then locating your breath in your body. Rest the attention here for just long enough to let the mind stabilize, and allow the body to settle. If you find your attention drifting, remember that this is natural. In the tiny gap of time where you realize you've left your breathing, simply acknowledge where you've landed and return to the breath in the body.

- Moving into contemplation, allow the eyes to gently shut if they haven't already. Begin by taking a few moments to give yourself a brief internal temperature check—How's it going, right now? I recommend opening this contemplation with the question, "What does it feel like to be me?" As your thoughts arise, stay watchful of what the mind and body produce in response to this question. Continue to return to this question as your object of meditation. In the spirit of nonjudgment, I encourage you to notice what develops in this space without making it mean anything about you one way or another. You're simply taking inventory, collecting information, getting a sense of what feels alive for you today. The response might be pretty obvious; maybe there is a strong or tender emotion that you're coming into practice with. Perhaps the response today is subtle, not much of anything at all. It's all okay. You're just allowing whatever is honestly here to have space and time to express itself. Leave the door cracked open. Continue to return to the contemplation of "What does it feel like to be me?"

- After a bit of time, you can loosen your focus on the question and bring your attention to the body. Whatever is arising in response to this contemplation, notice if and where it presents itself in your physical body. Notice the felt expression of this mood or emotion. It might be worth spending a bit of time working with the felt sensations directly. Does this mood or emotion have a particular velocity, a way that it moves in your body? Perhaps it's speedy; perhaps it's a bit more still, or stagnant even. Does this mood or emotion occupy a particular space in the body? Does this space feel expansive? Contracted? Both at times or something in between? Does this mood or emotion have a particular density? Does it feel thick or solid? Perhaps it's more wispy and ephemeral? Continue to feel into whatever is sincerely present in this moment.

- In the moments that you notice yourself drifting from this practice, turn and look at your mind. What are your thoughts doing? Again, no judgment necessary. Perhaps you find yourself avoiding or analyzing the situation. I encourage you, to the best of your ability, to drop the narrative about what you might be feeling, and to return to the raw material itself: the felt sensations in your body.

- If you find yourself working with a strong, tender, restless, or inflamed emotion, and your demon material is clearly present, you might send your discomfort a bit of compassion as you continue to rest with it directly. Place your hands on that part of your body where you feel the discomfort, and silently say, "I see you. Thank you for the information. I love you." Notice how your afflicted emotions feel under the warmth of touch when you don't make them a problem.

- After some time, notice if your mood or emotions have shifted at all since you began spending time with them directly. Maybe they've grown or subsided or are something very different altogether. Again, there's no need to make anything happen here. You're just allowing space to feel your emotions directly.

- You can continue to practice in this way for however much time you allotted yourself. If you are still working with a strong, inflamed, or tender emotion when you're ready to segue out of practice, you might consider visualizing a beautiful box to gently place your emotion in. In your mind's eye, close the lid and turn the clasp, recognizing emphatically that you are not getting rid of your emotion; it is still wholly your responsibility. You're just keeping it safe until you can spend more time with it directly.

- In the final few moments of practice, allow the contemplation to drop and return to the breath in your body. Take a minute or two to rest here, feeling the body breathe as a way of bookending your practice.

9

Surrendering the Plan, Walking the Path
The Fourth Noble Truth

Leave the door open for the unknown, the door into the
dark. That's where the most important things come from,
where you yourself came from, and where you will go.

Rebecca Solnit, *A Field Guide to Getting Lost*

The Fourth Noble Truth is akin to a Russian nesting doll that,
once opened, unfolds into layers of practicum in the form of
the Eightfold Path. The path reminds us of the truth of personal responsibility; our lives are participatory, and the work
of alleviating our pain and confusion cannot be phoned in,
farmed out, or manufactured. Revelations require sweat equity,
and this is the good news, because it puts the ownership of our
lives squarely in the palms of our hands.

There's a wonderful parable about the Fourth Noble
Truth that begins with the arrival of new monks and nuns
at a Buddhist monastery. They would approach the abbot,
or overseer of the monastery, and ask for instructions about
the path of practice. Many of these monks and nuns asked
for a plan or a map, something tangible and neatly organized
that would give them a linear action plan for freedom and

enlightenment. In today's world, I imagine this as a resource packet or a BuzzFeed list like "Eight Steps to Changing Your Habits so You Can Finally Feel More Free," or something of the sort. If these newly arrived monastics were insistent enough, the abbot would acquiesce and point them to the literal "path" they were asking for—a narrow, overgrown walkway in a remote corner of the monastery grounds. He instructed each of these novices to follow the walkway, as they would find the path that they were looking for waiting at the end.

These new monastics would set off, intrigued and hopeful, walking carefully through the overgrowth and bushes. Before long, though, the walkway took an abrupt turn, and they found themselves blocked on all sides, face-to-face with an insurmountable mirror. Some of the monastics assumed that they had taken the wrong path and would retrace their steps, inevitably finding their way back to the mirror, again and again, as if they were in a labyrinth. Many assumed that the mirror was on the trail to show them that the real path was within them, not in the external world. This caused some to run away, frightened, and others to collapse hopelessly overwhelmed. Some felt duped and hurled rocks at the mirror in anger. The mirror would not budge, however, and the rocks simply bounced off and struck the monastics instead.

Some of the monastics were delighted to find the mirror. They gazed in admiration at their own reflection, delighted and mesmerized by what they saw. They fawned over their own reflection, absorbed by the notion that they were on the great Buddhist Path. And of course there were some who tried to bypass the mirror altogether, plunging headlong into the bushes only to emerge bloodied from the impenetrable web of thorns and undergrowth. Some of the monks and nuns only saw their mother or father, or a dense crowd of people, both of which obscured their reflection altogether.

After a bit of time with the mirror, some of the monks and nuns settled enough to look at their own reflection calmly. For many, it was the most intimate look they had ever given themselves. More than a few concluded that the mirror and their reflection was the end of the path. They ended up stuck there for a very long time. The others, however, had a wonderful realization: "This reflection is of me, but I am not the reflection." They then reached out and gently touched the mirror, which gave way like a swinging door. Beyond the mirror was a vast garden bathed in light. And there stood the abbot, smiling, holding two shovels and ready to get down to work.

I love this parable for a number of reasons. It reads like a pithy instruction manual of wrong turns, outlining all of the ways we can get tripped up or confused in our understanding of the Eightfold Path—all without righteous sanctimony. Confusion will happen. That's cool, too. The parable also pokes fun at our human desire for a solid, concrete plan with defined metrics of success and bullet-point action steps. While quantifiable goals can be helpful in life, that's not what this particular voyage is about. If anything, the Eightfold Path asks us to surrender the plan and to swim in the process instead.

This parable illustrates so well the many ways we react to seeing ourselves on the path. Some of us throw rocks at ourselves or collapse in overwhelm or self-absorption. There are those who dive into the bushes looking for a "hack" or a bypass so they don't need to confront themselves at all. For many of us, we do not see ourselves honestly at first. We see who we are through the eyes of others, obscured by the expectations of loved ones or the projection of how others might perceive us. It's only once all of these tactics and projections have faded that we can approach the mirror with clear eyes. In many ways this is the point of meditation. We sit down and see our minds reflected back at us, including all of the sophisticated tactics we use to haggle with what we find.

The Fourth Noble Truth is, above all, a path of continued inquiry. It's an open-ended question mark with our minds and our lives as the subjects. This, in my opinion, is what makes the path so juicy; nothing is closed off to exploration. Much like what the choreographer Twyla Tharp once said about her creative practice: "Everything is raw material. Everything is relevant. Everything is usable."[1] Insights have space to arise on the path because there are no definitive answers to be found. Everything is material. Something might feel unsettling about this proposition, especially if we consider ourselves linear thinkers who are accustomed to wanting clean, straight lines; we might like to avoid the nebulous gray area where paradox and many possible angles exist. If only life were that clean and simple.

In Pali, the native language of the Buddha, followers who walked the Eightfold Path all the way to enlightenment were called *Arhats*, which translates as "the worthy ones." These teachings suggest that there are ways of accessing our inherent *worth* while working with what obscures it—in a moment-to-moment, participatory, life-path sort of way. The Fourth Noble Truth respects that we are dynamic creatures living a multifaceted existence. It simply points out the Truth of things as a workable infrastructure and then lets us have our way with it. There is plenty of encouragement to stay open to exploring our relationship to ourselves and what we are experiencing.

Who am I in relationship to myself?

When do I undermine or advocate for myself?

What conditions coax my heart to open?

Where do my own barriers and biases shut me down?

On the path, everything becomes a learning process. However, with this learning process, there's no aftertaste of ambition to reach the answer or look for a definitive something. The path of continued inquiry encourages us to relax a little bit. A rule of thumb on the path is that questions open things, while answers shut them down. This can be particularly helpful to remember when it feels like we've run out of options. Questions can be crowbars that create windows where walls once stood. There is nothing to find and everything to explore. In this way we can see, taste, and possibly even rest in the worth of every experience, whether we find it enjoyable or not. There is no waste of time. Everything has merit. This is it. This is the main event. Right now.

The First Noble Truth clearly defines the harder truths of the human condition. There is something dissatisfactory about our temporary nature and the pain that we inevitably encounter. The Second Noble Truth highlights that our strategies for facing our discomfort are what cause and perpetuate our suffering. Dissatisfaction makes us ache for comfort and pleasure, which we latch on to for dear life. We confuse our pleasure for something everlasting and as the ultimate source of our happiness, which prompts us to lash out at any threats to it. Attachment, craving. Aversion, aggression. And so, the whole cycle keeps spinning.

The pivotal piece of the cycle is our deep-seated confusion, or the third root poison of ignorance. We don't realize that this cycle is spinning or who we even are without the things we identify with because our Buddha Nature is concealed.

Demon material abounds here in this confused state of mind of ours. The Third Noble Truth reminds us of our inherent worth and basic goodness, which promises an alternative to the cycle of dukkha. And the Fourth Noble Truth shows us how to reveal and then rest in the worth of all situations by inviting us to step onto the Eightfold Path.

On the Spot Practice

When a demon is demanding your attention and you are feeling frustrated or stuck, see if you can shift your view to one of practice. This very moment has something to teach you. You can come into your body, feeling the solidity and weight of it on the Earth. Rest here for a moment. Then ask yourself, "What can I learn from this demon?" This is the path. Again, this moment is the main event.

PART 3

The Eightfold Path

The Eightfold Path is a practice in wholeness, which is reflected in its form. It's an interlocking system in which no one aspect of practice takes precedence over another, but rather each one showcases the holistic nature of our lives. Everything that we touch in one area of our being reverberates in the others. Nothing happens in a vacuum. Everything is connected.

The Eightfold Path is made up of eight aspects: Beneficial View, Beneficial Intention, Beneficial Communication, Beneficial Action, Beneficial Livelihood, Beneficial Effort, Beneficial Mindfulness, and Beneficial Concentration. We'll be looking at, working with, and practicing the development of each, both on their own and in their inevitable intersections. The Eightfold Path offers us a holistic perspective of our life drawn from nature's playbook: as ecosystems are whole and complete biospheres of life in which nothing is wasted and everything feeds and nourishes everything else, so too are the different teachings of the Eightfold Path integrated in a way that everything involves everything else, and nothing is wasted.

The Eightfold Path is a way to connect to our self-worth by living in a way that draws it forth and exposes it. There is a philosophy of design that says the designer's job isn't to add more to create the piece but rather to gather all of the materials and strip away the extraneous until the design emerges. It's rumored that the great sculptor Michelangelo whittled away the marble that "wasn't David" when creating his sculptural masterpiece. In order to become a watchful custodian of the worth and dignity that resides in things, perhaps we have to coax that same worth forward in ourselves. This idea takes us back to the "basic botany" of the Venerable Robina Courtin. First we must notice our tendency to pick and choose what parts of ourselves we give credit to and what we dismiss as subpar: "Oh, this part of me is worthy, and dignified. This, over here, is trash." We can then apply this discernment to other areas of our life.

In many ways the Eightfold Path challenges us to stretch our understanding of this invisible binary that we operate from—worthy or trash—and the black-and-white thinking that can develop from the root poisons that obscure our view. The whole of the path might be boiled down to the practice of relating to ourselves, each other, and our society more consciously, and doing so begins with noticing the way that we sift our lives into binary piles: worthy/inferior, dignified/cheap, spiritual/mundane, sacred/profane. What if manifesting a dignified life begins with simply noticing where our lines are drawn and beginning to blur them all together? What do we place in the realm of the worthy, dignified, beautiful, and exalted? What gets diminished, denied, and discarded as waste?

10

What's the Story, Morning Glory?

Beneficial View

> But if you really learn how to pay attention, then you will
> know there are other options. It will actually be within your
> power to experience a crowded, hot, slow, consumer-hell
> type situation as not only meaningful, but sacred, on fire
> with the same force that made the stars: love, fellowship,
> the mystical oneness of all things deep down.
>
> David Foster Wallace, *This Is Water*

If I were to ask you to tell me a story about yourself, what
would you say?

Maybe you have a few personal favorites on deck. Perhaps
there's the story of the place where you grew up, your childhood home or the lack thereof, and how that reality shaped you.
Perhaps you would share family mythology and yarns of experiential ephemera that helped to shed light on your character—the
ones about the smell of gasoline on your dad's overalls after work,
kicking up mounds of leaves to forage for wild mushrooms in
the spring, the feral spirit of your great-grandmother, whom
you never met but family lore has it toured America in a Western
band. There are coming-of-age tales of getting dumped by friends
and kissed by crushes. Or that crazy time you took a road trip

to who knows where to do who knows what, and you returned home with a better understanding of yourself. Perhaps you would look at me blankly and shrug, suggesting that you don't have any stories worth telling. You don't fancy yourself a story-teller, per se. How many of us do, after all? Storytelling has been branded by many as a skill reserved for only comedians, novelists, and playwrights.

However, if I asked you how your day went, you would most likely tell me a story as a matter of course. Very few of us can help it. Stories are birthed to us by human design and reflect the wiring of our minds—right down to the way that we catalog our experiences in chronological order and then recall them in narrative arcs. We've maintained centuries of cultural identity and traditional practices by preserving them in neatly spun time capsules of mythology, fable, and folklore. *This is who we are as a people. This is what it means to be human.* As the writer Joan Didion once famously noted, "We tell ourselves stories in order to live."[1] We're swimming in stories, both societal and personal, and we're all living under the influence of our storytelling minds.

As we make our initial foray onto the Eightfold Path, the first thing that's being asked of us is to take a lovingly honest look at the stories that we tell ourselves, where they originated, and what we believe they mean. In Sanskrit, this opening aspect of the Eightfold Path is called *samma ditthi*, which can be translated as Wise or Beneficial View. Although the Eightfold Path itself is not linear, the location of Beneficial View as our entry point speaks volumes to its importance. Our point of view, or perspective, is as unique as our experiences, and it shapes our relationship to everything we encounter, including, and perhaps primarily, our relationship to ourselves. It's here at the outset of the path that we're asked to pause and take inventory of the stories, experiences, and beliefs that have shaped our outlook, and to discern which are helpful, which are harmful, and which were never even ours to begin with.

Consider this: Have you ever had the experience of waking up in the morning feeling like a blank slate? My meditation practice has equipped me with the wherewithal to experience this as a split second of true wakefulness before the daily download of my view begins. This moment is barely perceptible, but at times I notice it within that second it takes me to orient myself to the world. It goes a little something like this: *Bed. Window. Oh, right... This is who I am. This is the person sleeping next to me. This is what I need to do today . . .* Along with the raw information streaming in, of course, comes our relationship to our circumstances: our perspective, our point of view. *This is how I feel about being me today. This is how I feel about that person next to me, and their mouth breathing and their sleep face and their body temperature. This is what I'm most concerned about and why events in my life happened as they did . . .* Within an instant, my whole worldview is back online, as though my entire sense of self had only been temporarily suspended by sleep. Not far behind are often subtle but very real emotions of anxiety, excitement, contentment, and ambivalence, depending on the day, and then an instant reaction based on the felt emotions. *Do I fly out of bed? Hit the snooze button? Cuddle closer?* The answer is all dependent on our relationship to our experience and the story that we subsequently tell ourselves about what is happening in that moment.

Beneficial View is where the path begins because our point of view is where we begin; the origins of our relationship to ourselves and our world is in our perspective, and it influences the way that we participate in these relationships. One person's disgusting mouth-breather might be another person's irreplaceable slumbering angel. I know from experience that this same person might occupy either role depending on what happened the night before. Beneficial View points out that what we are experiencing is not nearly as important as our relationship to what we are experiencing, and herein lies our story: our personal narrative lives in the relationship that we map onto the raw information that comes streaming in through our senses all day long. Our beliefs and our preferences act as filters, categorizing each smell, sound, taste, and touch into categories of what we like, and what we don't. Very rarely do we interact with the raw material of our experience, but rather the way that we feel about it. Another way of saying this is that our world is subjective. Our stories live in our point of view. Meditation practice helps us to slow down enough to watch our narrative unfold.

The Limitations of Our View

One of our greatest handicaps as humans might be that we only have access to a single point of view. It's a bit like seeing the world through a single pinprick in a tapestry with billions of tiny holes. Each of us has a pinprick we look through that shapes our beliefs and opinions. We witness ourselves and the world through this view, which acts as our reference point. For some of us, at any given moment in time, the view is friendly, open, and spacious. Then there are those of us who may be witnessing the same events from a different perspective, who interpret the same events as dangerous or something to avoid or protect ourselves from.

Our pinprick on this tapestry is our *positionality*, our position in relation to other things. Any number of things can help to define our position on this tapestry and the view that we ultimately see. Our gender gives us a particular position in relation to other things; we view the world through the lens of what it's like to be a woman or a man or a gender identity that is more fluid because it's how we experience things. Our culture gives us a particular lens, position, and point of view. Our socioeconomic status, our skin color, our sexual orientation, our religion, our political affiliation. All of these varying experiences shape our position on the tapestry, and thus our view. Our view is shaped by our experiences, our relationships, our society, and where we find ourselves positioned within them.

The funny thing is, we tend to think that our pinprick in this massive tapestry is the only pinprick that there is. We situate ourselves in clusters and communities of people who have pinpricks very close to ours, which is a very primal thing. We feel a sense of safety and belonging when we're surrounded by other people who have a shared point of view. This makes a lot of sense: people who have a similar positionality experience the world in similar ways. We often feel like they just "get it." However, when our orientation to the world forms from encounters with only those who share our view in the tapestry, we can develop a very narrow way of seeing things. Our view is continually verified by those who share it, so we come to believe it's the only one there is. Or, at the very least, that it's the "right" one. We can easily fail to recognize that others are witnessing the exact same events from a completely different position, which naturally leads to a different view and interpretation.

After the 2016 election, there was a lot of talk about the "bubbles" that we started creating for ourselves with the advent of the internet. Sure, we have greater access to other people in different places now than we ever have before, but we still tend to organize ourselves in a very tribal way, connecting with others who share our singular orientation to the world. I witnessed this firsthand in a place I never expected.

In 2011 during the Occupy Wall Street movement in New York City, I was drawn to the tiny village that had sprung up in Zuccotti Park seemingly overnight. There was a volunteer-run kitchen located in the heart of the park that was feeding the occupiers, a donated library with books on diverse topics, a medical tent, and various teach-in clusters with free workshops. A multifaith altar had even sprung up around a tree christened the Tree of Life in a tiny corner on the eastern edge of the park. It's here that "spiritual" activities from all denominations took place during the encampment, including drum circles, prayers, and daily meditations that a few friends and I from The Interdependence Project took the liberty of organizing.

The unification that was occurring drew me to the park; it was something I had never experienced before. In this unique pop-up community of citizenry, folks from all walks of life were engaging in constructive conversation about a shared heartbreak: economic injustice and its many repercussions. There were street punks and professors, indigenous people, trust-fund kids, elders, blacks, whites, Muslims, Christians, transgendered people, elitists, Tea Party members, democrats, truck drivers, Southerners—people of every sort of identification and affiliation one could think of. In short, it was glorious—a vast array of pinpricks in this tapestry sitting down face-to-face and sharing and receiving each other's points of view.

A month into the occupation, after hosting a meditation at the Tree of Life, one of the occupiers shared with me his sense of a shifting in the park that he had noticed. "People have really started keeping to their own these days," he reported. Apparently within a few weeks' time, lines of division had begun to be drawn, with tribal clusters congealing around shared positionality. The "intelligentsia" were sleeping up toward the west side of the park near the library; they had begun to host sit-ins and workshops that felt exclusive to their group. The street punks had assembled a tiny village of tents on the south side. A group of "yuppies," as this occupier called them, had branded themselves the Upper East Side Sacks and had clustered together as well.

It was confusing to me to witness the quickness with which we had re-created tribal bubbles to include a "we" composed of people with shared points of view, while casting everyone else in the role of "other." Even on a seemingly blank and egalitarian canvas like Zuccotti Park, which showed so much possibility, this happened. In retrospect, however, it's not shocking at all. I imagine it's nearly impossible to change the world without also working with our view. We're bound to re-create our world based on the model that we have in our minds, which is what makes Beneficial View, or whole view, so interesting: as we get intimate with the source of our own wisdom and confusion through meditation, we can see the ways that we re-create our world through the same old dusty lens. We can see how habitual our view actually is. We have more choices to try things differently when we examine our stories. Our view becomes a bit more malleable, not so rigid.

The psychology term *confirmation bias* describes the human tendency to walk through the world collecting information that verifies what we already believe to be true. We disregard or, in some cases, are simply blind to information that conflicts with our view of reality. I've heard it said that humans are much more like lawyers than scientists in this way. We aren't impartial investigators. We've already made our case. Now we're just looking for information and witnesses to verify it.

Having a point of view and wanting to be with others who share it aren't necessarily unhealthy things. Commonality is the adhesive of communities and relationships. However, it is worth noting where our points of view and the stories that they feed us begin to feel a bit rigid, fixed, and stingy. This includes our view of ourselves and the subsequent stories that we tell ourselves about who and what we are.

Bigger Isn't Always Better
(and Other Cultural Myths)

Some of our beliefs aren't even ours. Like old wives' tales passed down through generations or reflected back to us through society, we inherited certain cultural and familial narratives, adopted them, and left them unquestioned as "Truth." Sometimes these inherited narratives and beliefs manifest as unquestioned traditions. For example, when making the Thanksgiving turkey, my friend's mother always cut the breast of the bird off and roasted it separately. This process was embedded in my friend's view of "how to cook a turkey." When she moved to New York and began hosting her own Thanksgivings, she also sliced the top off the turkey and cooked it separately. Naturally.

One year a guest asked her why she didn't cook the turkey whole, which got her to thinking. She didn't actually know why. It's just the way it had always been done. So she called her mother to ask about the tradition: Why do we cut the tops off our turkeys? Her mother replied that she had always taken the top off because her mother had always taken the top off; it's just the way she had learned how to cook a turkey. Naturally curious as to where this learned behavior all began, her mother called her mother, my acquaintance's grandmother, and asked: Why do we cut the tops off our turkeys?

The grandmother, stumped, thought for a long, hard minute. "Oh," she remembered, "the oven in my very first apartment was too small to fit an entire turkey, so I had to cook it with the top cut off." Sixty years later, in a city across the country, my acquaintance was still cooking turkeys as a result of an oven that was too small. This is how inherited narrative works.

Here are some of the narratives that I inherited over the years, in order from most helpful to least: You can be anything that you want to be. Money isn't very important. It is what it is, and it can't be changed. Men prefer pretty over smart. Asking for help means you're weak and needy. These are the ones that I've managed to tease out; I'm sure there are plenty more operating in the background that I can't see.

Part of developing a wholesome or Beneficial View is identifying the stories that we live by, where they came from, and, perhaps most importantly, whether or not they are helpful on the path of waking up to our worthiness. Shariputra, one of the Buddha's chief disciples, described Beneficial View as the practice of identifying which of our views spring from beneficial beliefs and which spring from harmful beliefs, and then choosing which to nourish and cultivate. Sometimes this also means looking at the views of the culture that we live in.

A few times every year, I host group coaching programs for a rather large online training institute with a global reach, drawing students from a dozen countries, primarily women of varying ages. These groups offer an encouraging environment in which we can speak openly about our fears and hesitations. Over the past decade, working as a coach has revealed to me just how many of us feel a chronic sense of falling behind and a nagging suspicion that we're not quite _____ enough. You can fill in the blank here with your own particular flavor of not-enough-ness. Not educated enough, smart enough, good-looking enough, likable enough, thin enough . . . You get the picture. A consistent element of these groups has been a gobsmacking number of women sharing that they view their capabilities as insufficient or lacking. Sometimes this feeling extends to the way that they view themselves as people. It's said that if one fish washes up on the shore, the scientist will call it what it is: a dead fish. Nothing of note, really. However, if hundreds of fish wash up on the shore, the biologist won't look to the fish for answers. They'll test the water that the fish are swimming in. So what's up with the water that we all seem to be swimming in?

In the Western hemisphere, there is a deeply embedded narrative of scarcity that is nearly invisible. I don't know about you, but I clearly remember playing the childhood game of musical chairs. It begins as a cheerful romp around the circle, with kids squealing and running to nab a chair once the music stops. As the game progresses, however, the stakes get higher. The chairs begin to disappear. The slowest, smallest, and most accommodating kids get disqualified. And the fastest, most aggressive kids advance amidst the dwindling resource of chairs. Good, clean childhood fun. Also, a wonderful way to implicitly teach kids this prevailing myth of scarcity: There is simply not enough to go around. And you better get yours before someone else takes it.

Author, activist, and fund-raiser Lynne Twist illustrates this phenomenon exquisitely in her book *The Soul of Money*[2]. She likens the scarcity narrative to a "helmet" of insufficiency that we wear throughout our day that flavors every interaction we have. For example, our first thought when getting up in the morning tends to be *I didn't get enough sleep*. As we get ready for the day, we think, *I don't have enough to wear, I don't have enough time, I don't have enough room on the subway, I don't have enough help to get this job done well, There aren't enough good men or women on Tinder, I don't have enough energy to meet up with my friends,* and then our final thought before falling asleep is *I didn't get enough done.* This view of not having enough is truly pervasive. It's no wonder that the women I've worked with consistently communicate that they don't feel like they can live up to their own, or society's, expectations.

Even if we try to address the messages we might tell ourselves about what we have and don't have, we can't avoid them altogether. I was riding the subway to Brooklyn one day when a father and his daughter, who was all of five or six years old, entered the train and stood toward the center of the car. She was chatting to her dad about her day at school until one of the many subway ads caught her eye. In it, there were two juxtaposed photos of a blonde woman. In one photo, the woman was frowning while holding a lemon in each hand, which were hovering at chest height. In the other, she was holding two grapefruits, also at chest height, but she was grinning. "Dad, why is she happy in that one and sad in that one?" the girl asked, pointing to the ad for breast augmentation. I swear the entire subway car went silent in anticipation of how her father would respond. He awkwardly and skillfully lobbed the question back to his daughter. "Well . . . what do you think?" The girl waited a beat and then answered, "She's happy there because she has big ones and sad there because she has small ones."

Clearly she had understood the message this poster was communicating to us all: a message of scarcity, insufficiency, and how one might always be "better." And in that instant I understood how conditioning works. *Hello, demon of self-doubt.* Just like the fish in the ocean, we're bound to swallow the water that we swim in. When considering what it means to develop Beneficial View, and the view of our own worthiness, it can be helpful to identify why we might not feel worthy to begin with. If our cultural perspective is rooted in the myth of "not enough," it would logically follow that we would inherit this not-so-beneficial view of ourselves. Through looking at our own mind in meditation practice, we begin to take stock of the stories and beliefs that are not serving us, unraveling this myth of "not enough," and revealing the Beneficial View of our innate wholeness and worth.

Experts Are Overrated

Now, if you have augmented breasts and you love your augmented breasts, then let me just assure you that I love that you love your breasts, and I would never intimate what a woman should or shouldn't do with her body. Lord knows that women have enough body shaming and inherited double standards around what we are supposed to look like to contend with. In fact, I'm not going to tell you what to do at all. There's a pretty good chance that we've never met, so to assume that I could tell you the best way to live, or which views are the best to have, seems a bit silly to me. Dispensing advice from on high is not my gig. I don't know you well enough. However, I very much trust that you do know yourself well enough, which is why I want to encourage you to begin trusting your own direct experience, including the wisdom within your neurosis, to make the right choices for yourself.

In the teaching called the Kalama Sutta, which I've heard referred to as the Buddha's teaching on free-will inquiry, the Buddha visits a town named Kesaputta that is inhabited by a people called the Kalamas. Apparently Kesaputta was a popular town for traveling sages to visit and give their teachings on the path of the spiritual life. In New York City, where I live, on any given night there are chakra attunements and kundalini classes being offered and Akashic records being read. I imagine Kesaputta was a similar, ancient access point for a variety of different teachings. By the time that Gautama the recluse, as Buddha was known by some, arrived to give his discourses, the citizenry of the town was thoroughly confused. The Brahmins, monks, and sages who had come before had all shared their teachings and why they were the correct ones, and why the other teachings were false. With so many contradictory viewpoints given, each one discrediting the others, which path of wisdom was the right one to follow? Did the Buddha know for sure? Rather than dispensing yet another perspective, he asked the Kalamas to investigate the truth of their own experience as the grounds for wisdom and understanding.

Had they found that participating from a place of grasping, fixation, and greed had set their minds at ease? Or had it perpetuated their anxiety? Had they found that attempting to eliminate their dislikes from a place of aggression brought them peace? Or had it perpetuated their anger and intolerance? Had they found that distraction and ignorance alleviated their suffering in the long run? Or had they simply helped to perpetuate its causes? I'm paraphrasing here, of course, to put some flesh on the bones of the root poisons, but you get the drift. Not unlike the Socratic method, the Buddha's method redirected the line of inquiry back to the Kalamas and encouraged them to be curious. Do these teachings align with your own direct experience? If so, how and where?

One of the hallmarks of Beneficial View is that it encourages us to commit to a view of curiosity and discourages us from looking to other people for instructions on the one correct view. Curiosity is generous enough to hold many viewpoints while keeping our own perspective supple. As Shariputra so cleanly framed the simple inquiry of Beneficial View: Is this view helpful? Or is this view harmful? There's much to be said about this kind of personal responsibility and choice. On the path to recognizing our own worthiness, beginning to understand and subsequently trust our own experience goes a long way toward helping us make friends with ourselves.

On the Spot Practice

When you wake up tomorrow, don't do anything. You can turn off your alarm, sure, but before you get out of bed do an internal temperature check: Lying here in bed, what is your relationship to yourself and to your day as you begin to enter it? Note any subtle emotions or physical sensations as you consider participating in the day ahead. Note any stories that you begin to tell yourself about what your day "will be" or "should be." This will give you some insight into your view. Is this point of view helpful or unhelpful? Is there any opportunity to drop the narrative a bit and simply rest with the raw material of feeling your body in bed? If you feel too underresourced or rushed to do this practice, bring to mind one thing you are grateful for: a loved one, your friendships, your health, even something basic about yourself, such as the fact that you have the use of your eyes or ears. Rest in any sense of gratitude for thirty seconds. Notice if and how this shifts your perspective. Then enter your day.

11

Motivation Made Lucid

Beneficial Intention

> Personal integrity or disintegration will of course be
> manifest in the tonality of actions and habits; nevertheless,
> it is the intentions, the capacities for choice rather than
> the total configuration of traits which defines the person.
>
> Amélie Rorty, *The Identities of Persons*

When I was a young design student taking theater classes in college, I received one of the most valuable lessons on intention from my Meisner technique professor, Mr. Price. Meisner is an acting technique based on staying penetrable, open, and sincerely responsive to what is happening in the present moment, so, in retrospect, it's not entirely surprising that this professor handed me tiny wisdom nuggets that have manifested in my meditation practice and on my path. While standing on stage, sheepishly reciting my lines during one rehearsal, Mr. Price's voice boomed from the audience. "Stop. Stop. Stop. Just stop talking, please." From the look on his face, whatever I was saying smelled terrible. He moved closer to me. "The most powerful position you can take on stage is to stand still. Look directly at the audience. And say absolutely nothing." I followed orders. "Now don't you dare open your mouth until you know why you're saying what you are saying. We would never go through the trouble of speaking unless there was something that we wanted. In order to play this character effectively, you need to know what that something is."

Beneficial Intention, sometimes referred to as beneficial resolve or beneficial thinking, can be understood as motivation that's made lucid, and the choice that exists for us in that lucidity. As Mr. Price pointed out in my scene study class, human beings always have some sort of motivation—even if we're not entirely sure what that motivation is. There is a reason why we communicate, or don't communicate, or roll out of bed and leave the house, or choose to stay in bed. This isn't even unique to our species; all living beings have a motivating force behind their action or inertia. For many beings, humans included, this motivation can be boiled down to the binary of the root poisons of attachment and aggression. We want to move toward what is pleasurable, and we want to avoid what is uncomfortable. This is pretty simple and primal and doesn't require much consideration on our behalf. However, as Mr. Price brought to my attention, things get really interesting when we consider the infinite ways that we go about strategizing how to get what we want while trying to avoid undesirable outcomes. Sometimes what we want is lovely and benign. We want to connect, to be seen, to make a living, to share love, to contribute. But we always want something to happen, otherwise we wouldn't bother saying yes. Showing up. Making the effort. For the most part, we're always trying to rearrange our experience so that we can have the experience that we want to be having. Even nonaction is motivated by something. The tricky news is that we rarely stop to examine what that "something" is, much less choose our motivation, or take the time to understand if it will honestly make us happy in a sustainable way. Our motivation is always there, but it isn't necessarily intentional.

Cultivating Beneficial Intention is different from setting goals. The words *goal* and *intention* have been used interchangeably so often that it can be easy to conflate the two in our mind. A distinction that I find helpful is that a goal is something that we can literally schedule in our calendars at 2:00 p.m. on a Tuesday afternoon and then show up and do, whereas an intention is more like the soft underbelly of a goal. Goals are quantitative. They can be measured and acted upon. Intentions are qualitative; they're more of a felt aspiration.

Along the same lines, if you've ever said yes to something, scheduled it in your calendar, and then showed up and noticed a subtle aftertaste of resentment, it may be a case of misplaced intention. Perhaps you forgot why you said yes in the first place, and then it just seemed like someone was making you do the thing. This of course is never the case. Even if our choices are limited, and none of our options are great, we always have a choice. A large part of the path of self-worth is placing ourselves squarely back in the driver's seat and recognizing our agency. Cultivating Beneficial Intention is, in part, a practice of owning our choices, and making them deliberate.

Intention Isn't Impact

While the one-two punch of elucidating our motivation and choosing our intention is a powerful combination, it isn't a magic charm that will make the situation that we're engaged in turn out to our liking. We can show up and participate with the most openhearted intent and still be misunderstood, turned away, challenged, or taken to task. The thing is, we are human beings, and we have blind spots. All of us. They are called blind spots because we cannot see them, and we cannot eluci-date motivations that we are unable to see. There are recesses of our psyche where inherited and acquired views live—the demon material of unconscious biases, unpacked privilege, and repressed trauma—that prevent us from extending grace or even knowing that we might be harming others with our actions. I want to assure you that this is both okay and also not okay. It may not be our fault, but it is our job to take responsibility for the harmful impact that our blind spots can create.

Early on in my teaching days, I told my class a Buddhist chil-dren's story about a farmer and his horses. Admittedly, I ad-libbed the story to the best of my memory and didn't credit where I had read it. After class, a Chinese-American woman pointed out how unsettling it had felt to hear someone who had no connection to her culture regurgitate a well-known Chinese children's story so care-lessly. She asked if I even knew the farmer's name or the origin of the tale, and I had to admit that I didn't. At first, I was taken aback. I had only good intentions for telling the story; I wanted to share an allegory that might be useful to others. However, the impact was cultural appropriation. This is how blind spots work. As a medita-tion teacher I had unintentionally harmed a student by sharing a story that I did not realize was not mine to share. In this case I could only vow to educate myself and make the effort to do better.

It takes the courage of personal responsibility to admit when we are wrong and vow to learn and do better. This is one of the places where Beneficial Intention meets Beneficial View. If we can keep a soft, pliable, and resilient enough view that is curious and open to learning, then we don't have to protect our positions as much. Our self-worth isn't so dependent on our identity as somebody who is "right." Nor do we so quickly internalize being "wrong." We're able to make space for our blind spots, learn about them, and stay curious.

 Take a seat and connect with your body's breathing, as you do in shamatha meditation. After two to three minutes ask yourself, "What is the quality that I want to bring to my day? How do I want to show up for myself and others?" Notice whatever answers arise and then repeat the questions. After two to three more minutes, see if one quality feels most significant to you. See if you can rest in that quality, turning your attention to simply feeling it. Then reenter your day, bringing this perspective to any demons you encounter.

Mind Meets World

Beneficial Communication

If there were no speaking or writing, there would be
no truth about anything. There would only be what is.
Susan Sontag, *The Benefactor*

On the Eightfold Path, *samma vacca* is often interpreted as
Wise Speech or Beneficial Speech, which in the Buddha's day
was probably a very complete definition as there were few ways
of passing along information, and the spoken word was the
primary vehicle. It's estimated that the Buddha's teachings
were passed down through oral tradition until being tran-
scribed close to five hundred years after his death, so it makes
sense that so many of his teachings are catalogued in num-
bered lists to serve as simple mnemonic devices for memory
retention and retrieval. To heap all correspondence under the
banner of "speech" was very de rigueur. However, cut to 2,600
years later, where we find ourselves inventing new ways to share
information almost daily: Slack channels, Snapchat, emojis.
For this reason, let's expand and modernize the definition of
samma vacca and call it Beneficial Communication, which is
more inclusive of all of the ways that we correspond with one
another in the digital age.

Communication, let alone Beneficial Communication, is tricky. On any given day, we have a few dozen opportunities to be completely misunderstood. We might consider the likelihood of this unfortunate phenomenon on a Venn diagram that includes how many people we come into contact with, how aware we are of our own needs and desires that day, and how many digital devices are involved in our communication process. At the intersection of these factors lives misunderstanding. Even in those instances when we're feeling present and self-aware while face-to-face with a friend who knows us intimately, lapses in communication are bound to happen. A teacher of mine once commented that it's a miracle that any of us are able to understand one another at all, citing that speech is the process of sound waves leaving one person's cute little mouth hole, traveling through the molecules of space, and meeting another person's cute little earholes. Just the physics of this exchange is baffling, let alone our ability to then interpret these sound waves in the way the other person intends us to.

After we've received these sound waves and identified them as a familiar language, we then assign these words meaning, largely based on our point of view and intention. Our internal filters are quick to apply an interpretation. *What does this mean? Is it for me or against me?* This all happens in the span of a millisecond without much thought or conscious effort, and the whole process is casually called conversation. The same goes for interpreting these shapes that are organized in tidy lines across this page: it happens quickly, with one's filters involved. It's a strange thing to be choosing words and thoughts to share with you right now with zero idea of how your cute little eyeballs, zipping across the page, will interpret them. Again, baffling. Of course, on the flip side of the trepidation we might feel about being misunderstood is the joy of feeling truly heard and fully received when a conversation really clicks. Communication can be as much a source of connection as it is confusion, which leads us to the communication that doesn't even involve language.

A widely cited series of tests on nonverbal communication performed back in the 1960s by Albert Mehrabian, professor emeritus of psychology at UCLA, suggests that when communicating our feelings and attitude about something, our physical cues count for 55 percent of the message, and our tone of voice accounts for 38 percent.[1] The words that we're using to transmit our feelings? They account for a measly 7 percent of our message. Mehrabian's research suggests that even if we're choosing our words carefully, our interior dialogue is on display, to the tune of 93 percent. Anyone who's watched a loved one mope about with arms crossed while asserting that they are "fine" and "nothing is wrong" has seen these findings in action. What's honestly arising for us has a tendency to trickle out despite our best efforts to be inscrutable—think "wearing your heart on your sleeve" or a poker player's "tell." We send physical and tonal cues that reveal our interior lives, which we might also call reading someone's "vibes." We're in continual communication with the world at large without even needing to open our cute little mouth holes.

This finding dovetails with the understanding that samma vacca, or Beneficial Communication, is that sweet intersection where mind meets body, which in turn meet the world, transmitting our view and intention to others. Up until this point on the path, our interior life—our view and orientation toward the world, our beliefs and preferences, our intentions—has been our business and our business only. However, the moment we come into contact with another being, communication begins, and all of our mind-stuff comes to the surface. This makes samma vacca an especially delicate arena. It's where our perspective begins to reverberate in the world.

The living inquiry for us in the realm of communication might be this: Can I speak in a way that recognizes and enriches the dignity of this situation? Or, How can I share in a way that uplifts myself and others? Sometimes, on those days when we've just gotten bad news or are feeling especially rotten, the question might just boil down to this: Can I hold this thought and feeling without throwing them at others? Taking a pause before discharging a sour interior onto another person can save us a whole lot of embarrassment and backpedaling in the long run. Beneficial Communication is a practice of finding our voice, trusting it as a vehicle of participation in the world, and using it with intention.

The Five Gates of Speech

The good news for us is that the Buddha clearly left a few guideposts for speaking wisely, confidently, and with the inherent worth of ourselves and others in mind. In the Vacca Sutta, we find the Buddha gathered with his monks sharing the five keys to Beneficial Communication, or the five Gates of Speech.[2] A statement that's endowed with these five factors, he taught, is well-spoken, blameless, and faultless. So, what are they? A statement that incorporates the five Gates of Speech is one

> that is spoken at the right time,
>
> that is spoken in truth,
>
> that is spoken affectionately,

that is spoken beneficially, and

that is spoken with a mind of goodwill.

Of course, because the Buddha said these qualities of communication were blameless and without fault, it's inferred that he also meant "blameless to ourselves"; when we're communicating with these Gates of Speech in mind, we don't have to spend so much time rehashing our conversation or wondering how it was received by others. The Gates are a helpful guide for communicating confidently. We're the ones whom we reckon with at the end of the day, and to feel good about the way we are connecting with others can give us a sense of assuredness in our interactions. The five Gates of Speech are checkpoints of sorts. They form a pithy and simple instruction manual. To paraphrase the Vacca Sutta: Just communicate the truth and that which needs to be spoken. Gently. With skillful timing. Let's look at the gates more closely.

Is Now the Best Time?

When and where am I communicating?

It's best to do an internal temperature check before speaking: Have I processed my emotions like a self-aware adult or am I on the verge of a tantrum? If it's the latter, please don't shame yourself. We've all been there. The first Gate of Speech encourages us to wait a beat before proceeding. One of my greatest challenges has been working with the impulse to say something the instant that I feel it. It's like my emotions form a smoldering nugget of language on my tongue that needs to be released immediately lest it burn a hole straight through my jaw, especially if the language formed in anger, frustration, or righteous indignation. Guess how often chucking my wrath at others has made me feel more connected to myself and others? Rarely. Guess how often I've regretted it? Nearly always. About twenty minutes after the initial satisfaction fades. Like clockwork. Part of choosing the timing of our communication is about digesting, or at the very least recognizing, our own emotions before expressing them, especially if they're hot. Sometimes this just means taking a breath to find words that are honest (for example, I'm scalding and confused right now) and that still uphold the dignity of the situation.

It's also important to choose the platform that best suits the message and is more likely to help it be well received. For example, if we're attempting to communicate the importance of spaciousness in a rambling, frenetic email, we may have lost the point. Similarly, telling someone that we love them for the first time will translate differently if it's sent via text than if it's shared in an intimate face-to-face moment.

The tricky thing about digital communication in general is that we lose both subtext (intention) and body language in the exchange; theoretically if these two factors account for upward of 93 percent of emotional communication, then we're taking a huge leap of faith believing that the meaning behind our words will translate having passed through the digital realm (emojis only go so far to bridge the gap). How many times have you sent a text or DM that wasn't received in the way that you meant? I've seen email chains escalate into full-blown arguments because it's so easy to make false assumptions about meaning when subtext isn't provided. Oftentimes a five-minute phone call can de-escalate an argument completely. Choosing a medium that communicates "I respect you enough to hear your voice and connect directly" speaks twice as loud as an email highlighting all of the reasons why we care.

Lastly, picking our timing is key to Beneficial Communication. Doing so can be as straightforward as feeling out the situation. I'm the queen of asking my husband an important question about our future when he's walking out the door for work, or of texting him options for cat-scratching towers when he's at a meditation retreat. Without consideration, the timing of our communication can make zero objective sense. If one chooses to deconstruct their deepest psychological traumas at a frothy dinner party with peripheral acquaintances, one might subsequently feel badly that the subject was changed and their feelings were rebuffed. The question of timing, like all skillful communication, should take into account this question: When and where will what I have to say stand the best chance of being received?

Am I Communicating the Truth?

What am I communicating?

A few years ago, the Venerable Dr. Pannavati, a Theravada nun, was a guest teacher at The Interdependence Project. When asked for her most important piece of advice for us, she didn't hesitate: "Be clear on what you know. Be clear on what you don't know. Speak fearlessly to both." This advice hit a particular chord with me, as it's the perfect antidote for hedging, which I'm prone to doing. *Hedging* is the type of speech that we use when we're afraid of being direct, either for fear of being wrong or because stating the truth plainly might be considered rude. Not to gender generalize (I'm hedging), but studies have shown that women are more likely to hedge their statements with words and phrases like *possibly*, *kind of*, *it could be* . . . and to use other tentative linguistic markers, such as qualifiers (sort of, kind of, a bit), tag questions (This wine is delicious . . . isn't it?), and filler language (I mean, totally). Take that information as you will.

When it comes to communicating the truth, or as the Venerable Pannavati said, "what you know," I would like to propose a distinction between the Capital-T Truth and the truth of our experience. Both are completely valid. However, they serve very different functions and can make our communication confusing when we get them confused. The Capital-T Truth is irrefutable, infallible, and has been subjected to objective testing. Gravity? Capital-T Truth. Sound particles traveling through space? Capital-T Truth. The Van Dammer at Milkflower in Queens being the best slice of pizza in NYC? The truth of my experience. (And, arguably, that of many others.)

The Capital-T Truth is a conclusion that many objective observers could arrive at despite their biases. We could say that the Four Noble Truths are Capital-T Truths; the Buddha didn't make anything up, he just pointed out the way things are. The truth of our experience is more of a point of view; it's informed by our beliefs and opinions—which are deeply valuable. However, when we forget this distinction, things get sticky. When we treat our beliefs and experiences as though they are the Capital-T Truth, we create the perfect petri dish in which bigotry, arrogance, and self-righteousness can develop. We forget that others may have their own interpretation or lowercase, experiential truth, which is equally valid (even if we consider it seriously confused). Communicating the truth often means leaving room to accept that not everyone would agree, and, frankly, that's okay. Ensuring that we are clear on which truth we're communicating—Capital T or lowercase t—can do wonders for helping us speak fearlessly to what we know in a way that creates space for other experiences and ultimately fosters connection.

Am I Communicating Gently?

How am I communicating?

His Holiness the Dalai Lama is frequently quoted as saying, "Be kind whenever possible. It is always possible." This statement is a gauntlet throw-down for those moments when goodwill and grace evade us. When we're surrounded by our loved ones and chosen familiars, it's often easy to speak to them with kindness. *I like you. You're like me. I see your foibles, and I forgive you.* However, this Gate of Speech of communicating affectionately becomes a true practice when we encounter those who installed our buttons to begin with (frequently our family members), or those who push them anew somewhere on the spectrum between annoyance to full-blown hostility.

Take Facebook, for instance, one of the charnel grounds of practicing the path of our self-worth. In our current political climate, I've watched it devolve into a strange forum where call-out culture flourishes and insults escalate quickly. It's as though all tolerance and kindness get checked at the curb when someone we're not looking at directly expresses a view that we don't believe. I also want to recognize that as a nice cisgendered heterosexual white lady, no one has ever questioned my right to exist. Also, there is a lot of justified anger in the world, which is why this Gate of Speech is such a radical challenge for a human being. It asks, Can you speak the truth in a way that is kind? Can you say what you need to say in a way that respects other people's basic dignity? Especially if you don't agree with them?

Author, activist, and former presidential appointee Van Jones coined the phrase "calling one another up"[3] as an antidote to calling each other out. It provides us with a bit of insight into how to practice speaking the Truth (or the truth of our experience) in a way that is gracious and gentle. Whereas calling one another out is frequently divisive and shaming and creates hard lines of us versus them, calling someone up extends an invitation of sorts. Calling someone out looks like the point-blank statement "You're a dummy," whereas calling others up involves taking the time to explain and look for lines of connection. It's an approach that says, "I completely disagree with you, and I also recognize that you're a sufficient and intelligent human being who is flawed like me and capable of change. I cannot comprehend your position. However, I'm open to understanding. I believe that you can do better. Can we openly exchange conflicting perspectives in the spirit of finding some common ground?"

Speaking gently and extending gracious communication is, in and of itself, an act of recognizing the inherent worth and wholeness of others—even and especially the ones whom we disagree with or think are acting ignorantly (from the truth of our experience).

Is What I'm Communicating Beneficial or Detrimental?

Why am I communicating?

One of the primary ways to evaluate our communication is to first check our intention for communicating. Does this message need to be sent? And if so, for what purpose? Most of the time we won't have a profound reason for sharing with others, beyond a desire to connect, to relate, to experience the kinetic exchange of friendship. However, even then it can be helpful to understand what we're choosing to connect over and how that shapes the dynamic of the connection. Do my words elevate or diminish the situation? Or is my intention here to prove, preserve, or protect myself?

In the traditional context of Beneficial Communication, the gate referring to the beneficial nature of what is being said applies especially to gossip. Now trust me, I love some juicy word of mouth as much as the next person. I have a border-line Pavlovian response when gossip is dangled in front of me: dilated pupils, salivation, escalated heartbeat. There's a reason entire industries have formed around this titillating pastime. As I reflect on gossip, I think back to the countless jobs I've had—both in bars and in yoga studios alike—where the sense of shared connection among the employees hinged on their mutual dislike of someone else, interpersonal theatrics, or who knew what about so-and-so. In all of my years, I have yet to see gossip create an uplifting environment. In retrospect, gossip was more like a weird verbal virus we all passed around. Identifying strongly with what we're against rather than what we are for leaves an icky psychic residue that smacks of the Three Root Poisons and never scratches the surface level of communication.

Conversely, we can use our communication to express deep sentiment, even if what we're trying to communicate may be hard to hear. Sometimes what's worth saying isn't easy, but it definitely needs to be said. I've had plenty of difficult conversations that fall into this bucket of both necessary and hard. Fierce and also compassionate. There are the conversations in which we set boundaries, communicate our needs, draw a few lines in the sand. A pivotal part of practicing self-worth is teaching people how we expect to be treated. We can do this in a way that is gentle, of course, but sometimes it's necessary for our limits to be spelled out. There are the conversations of confrontation with loved ones who we can see harming themselves through their actions. True compassion isn't about watching someone flop around in their own confusion because we want to appear "nice." Sometimes love means pointing out the hard truth while reaching out a hand to either pull the person up or to create some distance out of respect for ourselves. Of course, even when we speak from a place of love, there is no guarantee that our advice or assistance will be taken. If these are the conditions that we place on whether we offer help or not, then the offer probably wasn't about being of benefit to the other person to begin with.

One simple way to check out whether we're practicing communication that is rooted in our sense of worth is to take an honest look at why we're saying what we're saying. What is my motivation here? For whose benefit am I saying this? We might find that questioning what's worth saying gives us the courage to be more sincere. We might also find that what we have to say doesn't always improve on the beauty of silence, and thus it doesn't pass the gate that inquires about its benefit.

Are My Intentions Good Spirited?

Am I the best person to deliver this message?

The fifth Gate of Speech is a final internal temperature check on our intentions, as if to double-check our work before handing it in. It may be that what we have to say is honest, gentle, relevant, and timely, but just to be sure, it's helpful to ask yourself this: Am I saying this in the spirit of goodwill? Or is there still a little bit of malice on my tongue?

In modern teachings on the Gates of Speech, I've also heard this Gate interpreted as "Am I the best person to deliver this message?" This is great question. Sometimes (and particularly in difficult circumstances) we will simply not be heard. No matter how kind. No matter how intentional. No matter how rooted in the Truth or the truth of our experience we are. We're just not the right person to say it.

When we're not the right person to deliver the message, it often has a lot to do with proximity. Perhaps I'm too far removed from the situation for my input to make an impact.

Oftentimes, I'm simply too close, especially when it comes to lovers and family members. Because our dynamics may already be established in a certain way (*ahem*, karma), no matter how I share my point of view, I will come across as a nag. Or a know-it-all. Or a silly girl. However, if a stranger or a business partner were to share the very same perspective, the message might hit home in a meaningful way.

Conversely, sometimes we're the only ones who can deliver a message in a way that another might hear. In the broader, societal scope, consider the kids from Marjory Stoneman Douglas High School, who galvanized a movement for gun reform in the United States of America. Although the conversation about school shootings has been on our cultural table for some time now, this is the first time a call for action came directly from the kids themselves. The truth of their experience has been so undeniable, gut-wrenching, and beyond the binary of political agenda that many of us are now communicating about this debate in a brand-new way. Both proximity and intention can shift the way our communication is received.

On the Spot Practice

COMMUNICATING WITH OURSELVES
It can be useful to practice bringing our attention to the words that we use to represent ourselves, both in our own mind (again, meditation) and, inevitably, in the world. Self-defeating language (like calling ourselves mean names) and talking down to ourselves are incredibly common habits of speech. Even if we're engaging in these habits for reassurance or to garner compliments, they are sticky practices that undermine our efforts to tap into our inherent worth. For example, last year when I traveled back to my hometown for the holidays, I

couldn't help but notice that my twelve-year-old cousin had taken up the habit of saying "I'm sorry" after asserting her thoughts and opinions. It's a habit of speech, yes, but one that's indicative of a larger belief at play—that is, "I'm not worthy of taking up space." Heartbreaking. In my cousin's case, we got to work quickly, breaking that habit by bringing gentle awareness to what was happening and by putting a quarter in a jar for me to keep each time she apologized unnecessarily for having an opinion. Incentivized awareness.

Over the next day or two, take note of your general communication patterns when it comes to taking up space in conversation. Pay particular attention to the words you use that represent yourself and your ideas and that express who you feel you are. Ask yourself:

- What habits of speech do I use when it comes to representing myself and my ideas?

- How do I respond to compliments, acknowledgments, and feedback?

- What language do I use to hedge, apologize, undermine, disclaim, and defeat myself?

- What purpose does this language serve?

COMMUNICATING WITH OTHERS

The great news is that we have endless opportunities to practice reflecting the worth of ourselves and others because most of us communicate with others multiple times a day out of sheer necessity. Here are two quick questions that you can ask yourself anytime you're about to speak, regardless of the medium that you're using:

- Am I communicating with the intent to connect?

- Am I listening with the intent to understand?

In our breakneck world of quick communications, passing through the five Gates of Speech can sometimes be distilled down to these simple questions. A couple of things naturally fall into place when we keep them in mind.

The first is that we're much more likely to nip miscommunication in the bud. This can prevent an entire rabbit-hole effect of hurt feelings and the resulting time that it takes to then clarify our intent. The second is that regardless of whether our communication is playful or more serious, communicating to connect and listening to understand quietly establish that you value the conversation that you're having and the worth of the person you're having it with. Who doesn't like to feel truly heard and understood? As Zen teacher Thich Nhat Hanh once pointed out: "Understanding is love's other name."[4]

Karma Made Me Do It

Beneficial Action

Some people need a red carpet rolled out in front
of them in order to walk forward into friendship.
They can't see the tiny outstretched hands all
around them, everywhere, like leaves on trees.

Miranda July, *No One Belongs Here More Than You*

In one of the group coaching programs that I host, we do an exercise called Story of Self in which participants tease out, from the tapestry of their life, the lived experiences that are most relevant to their livelihood. Like any traditional narrative arc, there is a beginning, middle, and end. There is also some sort of catalytic moment that either gently nudged or mercilessly body slammed them out of their previous status quo and onto the path that has led to where they are now.

Regularly in these group storytelling sessions at least one person will describe what I call their "spontaneous arrival." The trademark of a spontaneous arrival story is that we lose the richness of the events that occurred between our previous status quo and our current state of being. The dust that we kick up in a moment of change, the dirt that collects under our fingernails, the heartbreak, the wound licking, and the slow path of healing is bypassed for tidy resolution that fits into a sound bite. "I once was lost, and now I'm found" with no mention of the mess or the actions that made things messy.

Perhaps we feel embarrassed of the shit-storms that have made us who we are. Perhaps we feel we're culpable. In either case, while spontaneous arrivals imply that what we needed suddenly appeared to our shock and delight, an insight dropping from the sky is rarely—if ever—how things actually work. Nothing happens in a vacuum; we arrive at the place where we are in our lives either through unconscious, sometimes downright harmful actions, or through Beneficial Action—a way of acting in the world that is in line with our realization of our self-worth. If we look closely, there are always causes and conditions leading up to an event, and repercussions that follow. A plus B equals C, as it were. Even if an event or an insight seems spontaneous, there was a lot of energy and action leading up to the occurrence that put the seeming spontaneity into motion. From the Buddhist perspective, there is no such thing as "suddenly" or "somehow it just happened." It all comes down to karma.

The word *karma* has been misused so many times that it's tricky to bring it to the table without first unpacking it in a nice, tidy manner. In the Western sense, karma often is confused with the idea of exchange: If I do good deeds, then good things will happen to me. If I do bad deeds, then bad things will happen. I killed a spider, so slipping down the subway stairs and landing on my bum was my karma. Seems straightforward enough. There can be a real sense of karma as "we get what is coming to us" scorekeeping, but if that were indeed true, it would open the line of inquiry as to who we think is keeping score. Again, Buddhism is nontheistic, so it wouldn't be God in the Judeo-Christian sense. Perhaps some

Universal accountant? I just imagine a nebbish man with a slight build and glasses crunching my numbers on an ethics calculator in the cosmos. "Held door for stranger. Adreanna gets one point for good karma." Of course the idea is silly, because as reassuring as it might be in times of uncertainty to think that our karma scorecard will pull us through (while landing the jerks who did us wrong on their bums in public so that we can gloat at our vindication), this tit-for-tat way of thinking is not representative of karma at all. Much like the path itself, karma isn't linear, but rather sinuous and winding. It's more inclusive and holistic.

The most straightforward translation of *karma* is "action"; however, the term packs in such an array of implications that *action* doesn't quite do it justice. It makes sense that we've swept karma into our vocabulary rather than simply swapping it out, because there is no perfectly direct translation. For the sake of considering karma through the lens of self-worth, we might think of it as "habit energy" or our implicit memory—actions of body, speech, and mind that are so deeply ingrained that we don't give them much consideration. They are habitual, auto-pilot. Tying my shoes in the morning is as much a pattern of karma as is quietly telling myself that I don't know what I'm doing, slipping into my role in family dynamics, or habitually shutting down and withholding affection when I don't get the response that I wanted. Karma is the ingrained and unexamined way that we move through the world. If you've ever asked yourself, "Why do I keep doing that?" it's karma, baby, karma.

Growing up in Wisconsin, there was snow on the ground for half of the year, and many of my earliest memories revolve around winter activities, such as ice skating and sledding. We would flock to Iverson Park in particular after the first "sticky" snowfall in October with our sleds. When the season started, the fresh cover of snow was pristine and level, a uniform dusting over the hills for our sleds to track down. However, as the season wore on, the snow continued to fall, and we continued to trek up and down those hills, carving patterns into the deepening snow. By March, our sledding paths were so deeply sculpted with banks of ice built up around them that it would have been nearly impossible to try to steer our sled down a fresh trail. The paths were well worn and defined with very little room for deviation. This is what I think of when I consider the way that karma works. Our habits of mind are the deeply worn sledding slopes. It takes intention and effort to change our course. Of course there is always potential to change our course. It might take a number of tries before we gain any traction down those less well-worn pathways.

When I reflect on it, my most significant life shifts to date have sprung from a sense of feeling so sick or saddened or frustrated by my circumstances—stuck in those sledding ruts—that it made more sense to break my own heart than it did to stay put and suffocate. I have a hunch that as creatures of comfort, this is oftentimes the human MO. We stay where we are in life, love, and outlook because it is familiar and comfortable, factors that carry a lot of weight. Never underestimate the human imperative to feel safe. We can spend an unexamined lifetime seeking out and protecting what gives us this feeling even if it isn't always in our best interest. This, too, is karma, a deeply ingrained impulse that is executed in habitual ways.

Mind the Gap

In a 1955 episode of the American Western *The Lone Ranger*, once the day has been saved by the show's titular hero, one of the characters stops to reflect on the episode's events: "There's two ways for a fellow to look for adventure: by tearing everything down or building everything up. Somehow I like your way best, mister."[1] Similarly, it can be said that our actions, especially those that are unexamined, are either informed by movement toward something or movement away from something else. Building up or tearing down. Rearranging the furniture for a desired result. When it comes to karma, the actions that we take are often in response to old information. *I can feel him pulling away, so I'd better leave first so that there isn't the threat of abandonment.* However, if we're even able to recognize this, we're nudging the door open to a whole new world of choice.

The vast and rich Twelve Nidanas are the classic Buddhist teaching on karma. Though they deserve a chapter of their own, they can be summed up as a diagram that walks us through the stages of how karma forms: often quickly, with very little opportunity for deviation. It's a toboggan ride straight down the hill. There is, however, a point on this ride where we can gain some insight into how to shift our habit energy—a moment where choice becomes available to us to do something differently than we're conditioned to do. According to the Twelve Nidanas, after our senses make contact with the world, we're hit with a particular feeling. This feeling might be pleasant—a response to pretty sounds or the scent of cookies baking. This feeling might be unpleasant—a response to watching a cockroach crawl across your kitchen counter. We might even have a neutral feeling; however, we're apt to ignore whatever isn't explicitly pleasing or painful. Because of this feeling, craving arises—or, to use the language of the root poisons, we're hit with an impulsive desire or thirst. If the feeling that arose was pleasant? We desire to hold on to it, make it last, eat the cookie, hear more pretty sounds. If the feeling that arose was unpleasant? *Get that fucking cockroach away from me now!* Our mind latches on to the pull-toward or push-away responses with us barely even noticing. Our senses lead to feeling. Our feelings lead to craving, desire, thirst. Our desire leads to attachment or aggression. And so a new cycle of karma is born.

While it may seem obvious how our habit energy is established on this toboggan ride, we often hit the sledding slopes with a complete lack of awareness. Or, to use the language of the root poisons again, we do so against the backdrop of ignorance. The great news is that there is a gap in the middle of this escalation where we're able to replace ignorance with the fat wedge of our awareness, thus leaving space to shift our karma. In the moment after the feeling hits, and we receive that first impulse of desire, craving, and thirst, there is an opening for us to rest with our feeling without immediately acting it out. Of course resting with the itch, or the burning coal of jealousy, or the impulse to text them back and give them a piece of our mind is easier said than done. This is where meditation comes in. When we meditate we're actively learning to rest with what is arising without jumping to do something with it. Sometimes the most skillful action we can take is not taking any action until we're able to hold our seats.

Acting Our Way into Right Thinking

When we're hit with an impulse or emotional feeling that we know is especially charged, we can pause for a beat, or for a few moments, to let the impulse land and then choose how we want to respond from a more conscious and deliberate place. In the bigger context of our lives, this "gap" might look like contemplation, deliberation, rolling a thing around in our mind and examining all of its angles and possibilities. It's extraordinarily helpful (not to mention wise) to know what we're getting ourselves into so that we feel as solid and prepared as possible. With both short-term impulses and long-term pursuits, creating space between impulse and action can give us room to reckon with any demon material that might be present and allow unseen choices to emerge.

However, when it comes to leaning into the unknown and taking action with something big, I'd be remiss if I didn't mention that too much space and contemplation can act like quicksand. There's something sticky and cozy about "thinking things through"; thinking can mimic the feeling of doing something, of taking action. But to be clear, we're not. We're just thinking. Ideas are just concepts, and concepts are only question marks until they've made contact with the world. Right thinking, or understanding, evolves from having gathered new information—perhaps more information than we currently have. We need to know when it's time to leave the deliberation room, and it's often sooner than we'd like to.

On the Spot Practice

Here are some examples of when it's time to act your way into right thinking:

- *When your concept involves other people.*
Do not presume to know what your lover is thinking, what your clients are challenged by, what your friends are feeling, or what your customers want from you. Don't let your confirmation bias convince you that you "know." Assumptions are deadly in relationships, because you're not relating to real-time feedback. *Go ask them.*

- *When you notice that your thinking is repetitive.*
Backtracking? Thinking in circles? You're covering

the same territory again and again with no new insights. Chances are this holding pattern serves a great function—taking action is scary because visibility makes us vulnerable. I get it. So if you just keep thinking about something instead . . . trust me, this is the best way to suffocate your ideas, or, as Henry Miller said, "slaughter our finest impulses."[2] There are no windows in the deliberation room. Put your ideas into action and let them breathe, socialize, and flourish.

- *When you know the next best step.* Not the big picture, not the full plan mapped out in bullet points. That neatly mapped five-year plan is bound to change the minute you take action and the world gives you feedback, anyway. We only have a limited amount of information—that we've collected from previous experiences or research. How do we get more information? What needs to be acted on in order to be better understood? What's the most skillful action to take right at this moment? When you know the next best infinitesimal step, *go. Do.*

Work, Money, Purpose
Beneficial Livelihood

Before I can tell my life what I want to do with it, I must
listen to my life telling me who I am. I must listen for the
truths and values at the heart of my own identity, not
the standards by which I *must* live—but the standards by
which I cannot help but live if I am living my own life.

Parker J. Palmer, *Let Your Life Speak*

When it comes to Beneficial Livelihood, the Eightfold Path provides us some pretty straightforward counsel by outlining what work is beneficial to our development and what isn't exactly aboveboard. There are really no surprises here; the advice is what you might expect. Do work that is life-giving and helps others; don't do work that harms others. Specifically, the Magga-vibhanga Sutta cautions against business in the following trades: weapons, trafficking human beings, butchering and processing meat, intoxicants, and poison.[1] Even if a few of these forms of livelihood aren't outright harmful, there is the potential to harm (as with a gun), which still makes them karmically questionable.

While there is no one commanding us to behave in a certain way on the Buddhist path, cultivating Beneficial Livelihood is precautionary advice for us as stewards of our own mind. As with speech and action, livelihood is a very hands-on and active part of the path. It asks us to roll up our sleeves and work with the material of our daily lives as the fodder of our spiritual development. Money comes along for the ride. Business transactions come along for the ride. I personally find these aspects about livelihood on the path of practice interesting; they distinctly blur the lines between the sacred and the profane.

Of course gray area abounds in determining what livelihood is beneficial, and there are always exceptions. For instance, even though the Magga-vibhanga Sutta cautions against slaughtering livestock, many biodynamic farms cannot survive economically without slaughtering livestock and selling meat. These farms work to heal the Earth by respecting the local ecosystem and by practicing a view of holistic agriculture. Biodiversity is respected. Livestock manure replaces chemical fertilizer. Animals replace machines. Biodynamic farms are often small in scale, and selling meat is how they are able to exist as a viable business in the climate of big centralized agriculture. Through one lens, you might say it's skillful livelihood, and through another lens, unskillful. Both, neither, nuanced, and paradoxical. Nothing happens in a vacuum, and one must also consider context.

The list of questionable income sources for "contemplatives" can get very granular. According to the Samaññaphala Sutta, spiritual folks are advised against working in the "animal arts," which include palmistry, reading omens and signs, interpreting celestial events, casting horoscopes, reading marks on cloth gnawed by mice, and placing spells on spirits.[2] If I've just insulted your line of work, I apologize. I'm sure that your integrity is absolute when you cast spells on spirits. All jokes aside, I know and love some very talented, witchy women who make their living doing any number of these things and have been helpful to others in the process. From the Buddha's perspective, however, just as arms dealers peddle in the root poison of aggression, so do professional mystics peddle in the root poison of attachment. We desire assurance. We're prone to grasping at illusions, getting swallowed up by our own anxiety. We want someone to tell us exactly how things are going to play out rather than learning how to swim in uncertainty. Most of the time we don't care what's in the cards or in the way the stars are aligned or in how the tea leaves read, as long as someone can assure us once and for all that forces beyond ourselves are going to deliver the outcome that we want. This is what the Buddha called bullshit on. He considered it dangerous to give seekers false reassurance that allowed them to abdicate personal responsibility—the one ingredient necessary for true liberation. Like everything else on the path, we're asked to have a light touch with our livelihood and to bring it into our living inquiry. A personal temperature check we could give ourselves here might be this: Does the business I'm in contribute to my ability to hold my seat? Do I feel sincere in my intentions and confident in my efforts? Is there something unsettling about my work that's been left unchecked or avoided?

Let's Talk Money, Honey

You probably have a weird relationship with money. It's okay, most of us do. I know that's pretty presumptuous of me, as we've probably never met. It's also fairly tacky and gauche to talk about money in polite circles much less with complete strangers. Maybe that's the money story you were raised with. Or perhaps you were raised with the story in which you were always talking about money because there was never enough to go around. We tend to talk about what feels most relevant to us, and when the ends aren't ever quite meeting, you can bet that takes up a lot of mental real estate and airtime in conversation. As it is with other relationships, when it comes to money we frequently learn how to relate to it as a result of modeled behaviors, picking up the narratives that we witnessed as children. As we become adult earners, we might find ourselves fumbling around with our own pocketbooks—sometimes feeling anxious and stingy, sometimes reckless and loose. Even though money touches every part of our life, it's a wonder that so few of us learn to relate to it skillfully.

In a pivotal episode of *Mad Men*, Betty Draper, the first wife of Don Draper, the show's protagonist, confronts her husband about his mysterious past. In a moment of coming to terms with his background, she says, "I knew that you grew up poor. I see the way that you are with money. You don't understand it."[3] She wasn't speaking to me, directly, but in that statement Betty Draper read me to filth. It was one of the first moments that I remember giving myself a little grace for my clumsy financial skills. Of course I was terrible with money. Why wouldn't I be? It's an education that I never received. So, if you are tight, slippery, evasive, or unrestrained with money in a way that isn't always great, of course you are. Why wouldn't you be? If the way that you relate to money has caused you great shame or embarrassment, I love you. Me too. And I encourage you to offer yourself a bit of forgiveness. Like all the historical material we bring to our path, there needs to be an interplay of gentleness and effort in order for our relationship to our finances to feel malleable. We can cut ourselves a bit of slack for the weird money karma we've accumulated while also vowing to do better now.

For better or worse, money is the language of worth in a society underpinned by capitalism, and nowhere else on the path is there such a direct connection between our worth and our perceived value. We exchange our most valuable, precious, finite resources—our time, our energy, our life force, and our attention—for a currency that's more tangible. It's easy to understand, in a very linear way, how one might conflate their worth or the worth of others with the amount of money they make. However, investing our confidence in physical wealth displays a certain fragility, a lack of confidence in ourselves. Why would we pin the sum total of our value on something that is frequently out of our control? One economic down-fall can bring us to our knees as quickly as the Eight Worldly Winds can. Self-worth that hinges on the numbers in our bank account is flimsy and unsustainable.

On the other side of the money spectrum, however, there is a tendency to write money off as a necessary evil, something dirty, base, or greed driven—not spiritual. This is equally irre-sponsible, as it is a bit of a head-in-the-sand view. We live in a material world, where physical money carries economic and political power. We get to choose where we allocate our funds and support what represents our values. Why would we pre-tend that money doesn't exist and thus abdicate what fiscal power we do have? In the language of the root poisons, turning a blind eye to money rather than looking at it directly and leveraging it with skill is a form of chosen ignorance.

In the Dighajanu Sutta, the Buddha has a conversation with a layman named Vyagghapajja, who asks the Buddha how to create happiness and well-being in a life that includes a spouse and children, civic responsibilities, and business. In other words: How do we live well in the context of our every-day lives . . . if we're not renunciate monks who live in a cave? The Buddha's answer was very simple: Apply persistent effort. Stay watchful and aware. Cultivate good friendships.

Develop a relationship with your money: not too stingy, not too loose.[4]

Rather than compartmentalizing money as the sum of who we are, or a vulgarity we reluctantly participate in, we're asked to bring it onto the path as just another living inquiry. Where do I spend my money, anyway? How does that reflect my values, my beliefs? What are some stories I carry about what money is and what that subsequently means about me? What does it mean to interact with money in a way that feels sane and skillful? Learning to relate to money directly is another way of learning to hold our seats. There is a sense of confidence that arises when we show ourselves that we can wield money, rather than clinging to or avoiding it.

As with all of the aspects of our path, we can begin to explore how we relate to money most when our demon material is present. What are our spending habits like when we feel the most detached or isolated? How do we use our income to create the illusion of self-importance? What do we do financially when we feel the most scared and unsafe in the world? An entire practice of spiritual expression could be devoted to contemplating and working with wealth. How do we relate to wealth, and subsequently wield it, in a way that facilitates stronger connections? More compassion? Generosity? Contentment for self and others?

The Pitfalls of Pursuing Our Purpose

I consider Beneficial Livelihood a lot. I've centered my work as a coach around this topic for years. It's an easy access point for conversations about self-worth as the leaps from our relationships to worth, work, and money are small ones. These topics inevitably lead a lot of my students and clients to the subject of purpose. Purpose is not a new concept, but it's one that seems to be on our minds quite a bit these days. Purpose-driven books topped the *New York Times* bestseller list in 2014, with titles like *Your Life Calling* by Jane Pauley, and *The Promise of a Pencil: How an Ordinary Person Can Create Extraordinary Change* by Adam Braun. And ranking third in the top-ten most-watched TED Talks of all time, Simon Sinek's talk "How Great Leaders Inspire Action" asks us what "our purpose, our cause, our belief" is, urging 41 million viewers (so far) worldwide to connect with our "why." I've shared this gem so often that I'm responsible for at least thirty of those views.

On one hand, I find this turn toward purpose incredibly heartening. In a culture that traditionally values metrics of success, it suggests that we're asking ourselves how to live by our own standards, collectively elevating meaning over measurement. Many of us are consciously contemplating what we're built for and how best to contribute to the world. On the other hand, I can't seem to shake the feeling that all of this "find your purpose" business is somehow missing the mark. There's something incomplete about the conversation, and it's the small but mighty distinction between having a purpose and living a purposeful life. It may seem like a matter of syntax, but syntax is important. Drawing from the teachings of Beneficial View and Beneficial Communication, the way that we see things and talk about things reveals our relationship to them and, ultimately, how we approach them. Much like with worth itself, purpose is the difference between seeking the keys to redemption and revealing what's already there.

During my dilettante days, I would lay awake, fixed on the water stain above my bed wishing for some sort of map. I had tried my hand at acting and spent a year in film school. I wrote sketch comedy on the side, worked in food advocacy, studied design, and worked enough crappy waitressing jobs to redefine my notion of humility. The more uncertainty that I felt about my place in the world, the more my little self-doubt demon would nibble at my confidence. The more that I looked around at everyone else who seemed to have it flawlessly together, the more that my comparing mind would kick up my little demons of jealousy, fixation, and arrogance. Surely I was smarter and scrappier than all of them. Inflation born from deflation. I was in the crosshairs of worldly winds blowing from every direction. I had a passion for travel and yoga, but could that truly be my purpose? I'd always had a knack for organizing, but was this my soul's North Star? When given too much gravitas, finding "our purpose" can be frustrating, and at its worst, a trap of paralysis. (Think: staring blankly at the ceiling wishing that a water stain would give me insight.) If we truly have a calling, a single purpose in this world, what if we never find it? Are we destined to go through the motions, a half-lived vessel of unrealized potential? How terrifying to consider. *Hello, grasping and fixation born from the aversion of utter failure.*

Defining our purpose as a destination or a single-pointed direction bears a resemblance to searching for "the One." It's an approach that holds true to the binary of purpose versus meaninglessness, soul mate versus hookup, rather than asking how we can expand our sense of worthiness to be a more inclusive practice. Even if we do find our forever person, or the mission statement we can live by that fills our days with meaning, the question of whether we've made the right decision, or if we're missing out, might still linger. Even if we feel a sense of certainty, it's easy to attach the expectation that this feeling will always remain the same, which pits our hopes against the laws of ever-changing nature. This is First Noble Truth stuff. In my case, purpose was just another way of chasing that magical "someday" that precluded my self-acceptance.

If you had asked me about my purpose when I was seven, I would have given you a cockeyed stare, most likely because I was busy discovering the world through first-time experiences. Everything had purpose, from crickets to kickball to Paula Abdul. My understanding of the totality of purpose came much later, however, clicking into place during one of those crappy waitressing shifts. I realized that waitressing wasn't, by any stretch, going to be my forever career, and I decided to try an experiment. What if I tried treating all of this—even my fried-calamari smell and the ketchup in my hair—like it mattered? What might happen if rather than approaching this work like a sidebar to my life's purpose, I brought purpose into my approach? What if I was purposeful instead of waiting for purpose to redeem me? The answer is that I stopped looking for my purpose—the one I claimed ownership of—and allowed purpose to flavor my moments.

I can't help but think that rather than having a purpose, we simply have purpose. It's something akin to dignity or meaning, an inheritance of being alive. We can direct our purposefulness through clearly chosen intentions, but ultimately, like worth, it's a quality that we possess, not a statement, a job title, or a place that we find. My friend Marisa once told me a story of a Brooklyn subway booth employee whom she encountered almost daily. Each morning she would emerge from the train, and he would lock eyes with her and greet her warmly. They became familiar through their daily exchange—a wave, a smile, a connection. She told me that the joy he brought to his booth, his generosity of spirit, made her day. After some weeks of this behavior, she noticed that she wasn't the only regular commuter this tollbooth employee had a relationship with. Some mornings dozens of people would wave and stop to say hello to this gentleman on their way to the subway stairs. This man's purpose wasn't written on a raised banner for the rest of the world to see, but rather he connected to the world through the act of purposeful living.

All this to say that if you're on a mission to find your purpose, the good news is that you can relax. Purpose is already there and best lived through you. The way to find purpose is to apply it generously: to the crappy jobs, and the sleepless nights, and the hours stuck in traffic. If our lives are purposeful, then nothing gets excluded. Our moments, after all, only have the meaning we give them.

On the Spot Practice What is one thing you can do in your work today that would impact another human being for the better? If you're drawing a blank, you can start by asking yourself how you want to be known by people at the end of your life. As loving, generous, kind? Then focus on one of these qualities throughout this one day. You can write yourself a sticky note and place it on your desk, set a calendar reminder, or have a reminder pop up on your phone to remind you of the quality in question, such as kindness. By turning your mind to who you want to be throughout the day, as opposed to focusing on just one act you might want to do, you are more likely to benefit others and build a career and life based on something you personally find meaningful.

15

Accounting for Our Energy

Beneficial Effort

> If you are ready to accept the result of what you
> have done, that is the only way to be free from what
> you have done: to go beyond the idea of good and bad.
>
> Shunryu Suzuki, Dharma talk at the
> San Francisco Zen Center, July 15, 1969

New York City is home to some truly phenomenal street artists. In recent years the trend has been for these artists to secure commissions and other more legitimate outlets for their work, though rogue graffiti artists still sketch their signatures in NYC's neighborhoods. One such work that I've noticed scrawled on blank walls and subway stickers is a simple set of questions: Are you helping? Are you hurting? The answer, of course, is subjective. At the very least, by creating a mess that needs to be cleaned up, our clever graffiti artist is not helping the person who has to inevitably, and thanklessly, scrape these stickers off the metro. They may even be hurting this person. To me, though, stumbling across this reminder has served as a quick recalibration, orienting my view back to my best intentions and the Kalama Sutta and Shariputra's simple question: Is this helpful or is this harmful? This might very well be the simple contemplation for the entirety of the Eightfold Path.

Here on the path at Beneficial Effort we give Shariputra's contemplation a little bit of elbow grease. The Four Noble Truths offer us a sturdy architecture for understanding our experience, and then we're left to run the suggested wisdom of these teachings through the mill of our lives, stick our hands in the soil, and do the work—live that old trope that anything worth having requires effort and sweat. Most of the work of the path includes tilling the soil of our own self-respect, trust, and acceptance. The irony is that our inherent worth is the most natural state of being, as natural as Earth itself. Beneficial Effort is where we take a loving and ruthlessly honest look at where we're exerting our energy, and whether our efforts amplify or diminish the trust that we have in our own value. As Zen teacher Shunryu Suzuki is rumored to have said, each of you is perfect the way you are . . . and you can use a little improvement.

Prana Leaks

In the conversation about exertion, effort, and the application of energy on the path, it's worth mentioning that many of us are truly knackered-out exhausted. I see it all the time on the meditation cushion. The moment we find ourselves in a state of relaxation, our chronic exhaustion peeks through. When we allow space for every tamped-down emotion, thought, and physical sensation to arise and express itself, don't be surprised if overexertion and sleep deprivation show up to the party.

A number of years ago an article circulated that featured "before" and "after" photos of participants at a thirty-day meditation retreat. In the "before" shot they look like regular humans, and in the "after" shots they appear to be lit from within, like personified balls of equanimous light. I'm sure that the month of meditation played a role in their preternatural glow, but I've always suspected that thirty days of deep rest, adequate sleep, and the resulting reset of their circadian rhythm probably didn't hurt either. Yes, we are very tired people. Overexertion is the water that many of us swim in.

Much of the exhaustion that we experience is related to how we use our minds. When my smartphone was losing all of its battery power before noon, I consigned myself to the impermanence of all things and was on the brink of buying a new one, when someone kindly informed me that if I double-clicked my home button, all of the apps operating in the background would display themselves to me. Essentially, I discovered that every app that I'd opened on my device was still open, operating silently in the background, zapping the charge of my battery. All I had to do was swipe my finger upward on the screen to close them, and my phone was as good as new. When too many of our mental tabs are open, our batteries take a hit. This isn't news to me. I can wake up in the morning fresh as a bunny rabbit only to be laid out by noon when my mind is busy and I have a number of concerns operating simultaneously. The owner of a yoga studio that I used to work at called this phenomenon of our batteries draining "prana leaks." It's the sense that our precious life force, or *prana* in Sanskrit, is slowly being used up by background tasks. Avoidance is a prana leak. Disheartenment is a prana leak. Speedy busyness is an obvious prana leak, with frantic energy shooting everywhere.

In the case of avoidance, I wonder, have you ever considered how much energy it actually takes to actively put off doing something? Procrastination can be exhausting. I know that when I'm dragging my feet to address something, it doesn't remain undone quietly. It's a big, loud app that's left open in my mind and comes screaming to the forefront periodically to remind me that I have to have that difficult conversation, because the issue will not just go away on its own. It actually takes energy to keep hitting the snooze button on our important but infinitely postponed affairs.

Disheartenment gets right to the matter of how much energy is leaked when we don't feel good about what we are doing. When we feel no genuine energy or pull to show up for what we've said yes to, it requires twice as much effort to maintain our forced enthusiasm because we feel no reciprocity or return on investment. We are pouring our energy into something that simply isn't giving us energy back. Disheartenment can also occur when we are too attached to the outcome of our effort. Perhaps we force our effort because we have all sorts of assumptions and expectations of what we'll receive as a result. When our payout doesn't come as fast as we assumed it would, or it comes in a different way, or maybe not at all, we lose heart altogether.

Speedy busyness is a tricky prana leak because it can masquerade as accomplishment. From the looks of things, we are hustling and making moves; we might even receive a lot of praise for how many irons we have in the fire. However, this type of busyness can make us feel very disjointed and directionless, and oftentimes it leaves us depleted. We might notice these feelings most in meditation practice or when we lie down to fall asleep; there are so many mental tabs open that our attention feels restless and scattered. Thich Nhat Hanh tells a wonderful Zen story about a man riding a galloping horse. An onlooker by the side of the road asks the rider where he is headed as he goes speeding by. The rider yells back, "I don't know! Ask the horse!"[1] Busyness can be like this horse.

So how do we streamline our efforts and protect our precious life force from tendencies such as avoidance, disheartenment, and speedy busyness? There are three classic antidotes for these leaks: prioritize what is important, remember why we said yes in the first place (ahem, intention), and then commit enthusiastically to the process rather than the end result.

Practices for Protecting Our Energy: The Four Exertions

There's something sobering about remembering that our life will one day be over. Rather than allowing this very real truth to spin us into a panic, it can help us to collect our wits and connect us to the invaluable worth of our time. In large part, Beneficial Effort is a process of remembering that our energy is finite and then treating it as such. This is an ineffable and indispensable practice of self-worth, if there ever was one. We don't get to do all of the things. Not all at once, at least. So what is worth your elbow grease in life? Even if it's difficult?

In the traditional teachings, the Four Exertions are skillful actions that we can take when it comes to choosing how we use our energy. The way of applying our effort beneficially is fourfold, as the name suggests. Classically the Four Exertions are listed as guard, abandon, arouse, and maintain. The simple premise this teaching offers is that first we take stock of what we're spending the currency of our energy on and what that exchange offers us in return. If it contributes to depletion, overwhelm, shame, or resentment, we have to either find a different way of relating to it or find a way to let it go. Simultaneously we turn our attention toward what is life-giving, joyful, and worthwhile. This is where we place our efforts. What is helpful? What is harmful? And how do we protect our energy from leaking out as an expression of our own value?

Protection Practice 1: Set Healthy Boundaries (Guard)

You know who you are: You say yes to everything. You're accommodating and gracious and feel an enormous sense of guilt when you have to turn down an ask or back out of an obligation. You might even be overly apologetic in these cases because you don't want to appear selfish, or ungrateful, or stingy. You may try to do all of the things, and all by yourself, oftentimes doing none of the things very well because your energy is scattered. This leads to a sense of failure and disappointment in yourself that you fear others will share. It also leads to inevitable burnout and fried nerves and sensitivity. I know you, and I love you, and I'm here to tell you that your overexertion and speedy busyness are not doing anyone any favors. Least of all you.

If you see yourself in this description, let me introduce you to your new motto for Beneficial Effort: strong spine, open heart. The strong spine piece is key. Compassion for others doesn't mean assuming the role of doormat, savior, or martyr. In fact, just the opposite. True compassion is predicated on our ability to stand up for ourselves when the situation calls for it, to lovingly communicate our boundaries, and to give from a place of recognizing that the receiver is already capable, sufficient, and whole. Especially as we become more tender and open through the practice of meditation, there is an equal need to recognize our own thresholds and to honor these thresholds by setting firm and clear boundaries of what we can and cannot do, allow, and tolerate. If someone is wielding a proverbial knife, saying no and gently disarming them before they can cause harm is a compassionate act toward all parties involved.

In the same way, offering someone the last sip of your Slurpee isn't necessarily generous. It's backwash. Reinforcing your open heart with the support of a strong spine allows you to practice compassion from a place of genuine empathy without the aftertaste of resentment, superiority, or expectation.

Protection Practice 2:
Renounce the Weeds (Abandon)

You know who you are: Your bad habits are starting to catch up to you, even and especially if you've been doing them in secrecy. This secrecy, incidentally, is the breeding ground for the demons of shame, isolation, and feeling all around bad about yourself, which keeps the whole vicious cycle spinning. You might have a number of "life raft" habits that you engage in to temporarily soothe your demon material or just one really big, murky habit that soothes your demons temporarily but also threatens to take you down with it. This could be a series of lies, a harmful fixation, or a full-blown untended addiction.

As silly as it may sound, on the path to befriending our shadowy bits, it's important to recognize that even our bad habits and addictions have a beneficial intention. We don't do these things because we're bad people. We don't do them because we're lazy. These explanations don't leave any room for our complexity and only perpetuate the war within ourselves. We reach for our vices when resting with what is painful is too intense; they're a form of self-medication and self-soothing, like a snuggly blanket that can have some truly destructive and heartbreaking consequences. Aversion and fixation. Fixation and aversion. This is the stuff of Second Noble Truth territory, and the antidote is to renounce what is harmful. I know you. I love you. And owning up to our habits is a courageous decision to make. We recognize that our attachments and prana leaks are deterrents on the path of self-respect, and then we ask for all of the support and help that we need to change. Renunciation is as much about moving toward what we want to create as it is leaving behind what stands in our way.

Protection Practice 3: Till the Soil and Plant the Seeds (Arouse)

You know who you are. The schemer, the idealist, the daydreamer. I see you and I love you. Setting clear and steadfast boundaries combined with the renunciation of bad habits frees up some of our bandwidth to consider what we'd like to plant in the big wide-open space that is no longer being occupied. Perhaps we'd like to grow more space itself. This third practice of the Four Exertions is where we get to play with potential and aspirations. What are my intentions? How would I like to feel? What might I sink my effort into now to bring my visions to fruition? When am I the best version of myself and what do I need to sustain it? Prioritize the living daylights out of what you love. What tickles your heart and taps into your urge to be more generous, patient, understanding, and kind? Again, I don't want to drink from the bottom of your Slurpee cup. I want you doing the work that you need to do in order to feel more replenished and thus more organically generous. Treat your aspirations like they're worth something. Because they really, truly are.

Protection Practice 4: Amplify the Beauty (Maintain)

You know who you are: your mind naturally floats on over to what's going wrong or what needs to be done next. With this point of effort, the fourth of the Four Exertions, we're encouraged to take inventory of all that is beautiful in our world and all that is going well for us while giving ourselves some credit. I know that giving yourself credit might be difficult. Perhaps the idea of loving on yourself sounds corny. Consider this: You are reading these words. Your one-in-a-million, can-never-be-replicated mind knows how to receive shapes on a page, transform them into concepts, and string together a cohesive idea that I flung through the atmosphere in the form of this book. You also have a delicate and sophisticated emotional-processing system that gives this idea meaning and reference and then fact-checks it against what you know. You do all of this in the split of an instant without any consideration, and you doubt that you are amazing? Repeat after me: "I am an absolute miracle of a human being. Worthy, whole, and complete." Now, please, continue to amplify all of the beauty that you already are and dedicate your energy to what helps reveal it.

On the Spot Practice

Notice which of the Four Exertions you find yourself gravitating toward the most. Where is your energy being depleted, and how might you protect it or redirect it? Accounting for how your energy is being spent and choosing what to guard, abandon, arouse, and maintain offers a wonderful opportunity to practice trusting yourself. Here are some questions that might be helpful:

- What do I want to say no to so that I can create space for more genuine yeses?

- What do I need to say no to as an act of self-care and compassion?

- How can I say no in a way that is direct and honors the dignity of all parties involved?

- How do my harmful habits help me to cope, and what might be the demon material that lives here?

- When am I the best version of myself, and what do I need to prioritize in order to sustain this?

- What in my life is beautiful, compelling, or nourishing?

- What would I like to give myself a little bit of credit for?

Try your very best, and be gentle with yourself when you miss the mark. This is Beneficial Effort in a nutshell.

16

The Spice That Flavors All Dishes

Beneficial Mindfulness

> My experience is what I agree to attend to.
> Only those items which I notice shape my mind.
> William James, *The Principles of Psychology, Vol. 1*

Mindfulness is having an undeniable moment in our collective conversation right now. In fact, as you were thumbing through the chapters of this book, you might have seen the title "Beneficial Mindfulness" and felt a warm pang of familiarity. I find the widespread turn toward mindfulness thrilling. This popularity seems like a natural evolution, as over the past decade neuroscientists have been able to quantify what happens to our gray matter when we practice mindfulness meditation. The cells of the amygdala, responsible for the primal reactivity of the fight, flight, freeze reactions we engage in when we feel fear, physically begin to shrink. The cells of the prefrontal cortex, referred to as the "human" brain, associated with cognitive thinking, language, decision making, and emotional regulation, begin to grow.[1] I don't pretend to have more than an armchair understanding of how these things work. I am not a neuroscientist. However, I do love quantifiable, measurable, statistical data as much as the next person, and so it's no surprise to me that this hard-copy "proof" would create a natural inroad to mindfulness, expanding its reach among the masses. Advances in neuroscience, coupled with our ubiquitous digital connection, have helped to precipitate a pendulum swing toward more mindful living.

You can attend mindful business seminars and take a mindful knitting class. We're mindfully parenting, and drinking, and dating these days. The brand Earth Balance even makes a condiment named Mindful Mayo, sold at a health-food store near you. The flip side of mindfulness being everywhere—including on our sandwiches—is that we might have jumped the shark in an otherwise heartening movement. For this very reason, I find it helpful to establish a working definition of what mindfulness is in my classes so we have a sense of what we're doing when we sit down to practice.

The pithy and concise definition that I continue to come back to serves as a tiny instruction manual. Jon Kabat-Zinn, creator of the Mindfulness-Based Stress Reduction program, lays it out perfectly: "Mindfulness is the awareness that arises through paying attention, on purpose, in the present moment, non-judgmentally . . . in the service of self understanding and wisdom."[2] I appreciate the specificity of this definition for two reasons. First, it highlights that mindfulness is not something that we need to acquire or receive. It's a form of awareness that arises organically within us when we've created the right conditions and are paying attention in a specific way. We all have access to mindfulness just by virtue of being human. Much like worth, mindfulness is an inborn state that we can practice attuning ourselves to and aligning ourselves with. While cushions and incense and candles are nice, they're not actually necessary for developing a mindfulness practice. We already have everything that we need. Though having an ample cushion to practice on is remarkably useful.

The second aspect of this definition that I find so helpful is the final piece of instruction: "paying attention, on purpose, in the present moment, non-judgmentally." Now this is the real kicker. I'm not usually a betting woman, but I would put chips on the table to say that each of us has had the experience of paying attention on purpose in the present moment. A loud crack of thunder can drop us back into the moment. As can a compelling conversation or full-bodied flail around the dance floor. Any time we're absorbed in the flow, as it were, we're in the present moment. It's a gorgeous feeling of captive engagement when it happens. However, doing so without judging our experience or ourselves in the process is what really distinguishes mindfulness from run-of-the-mill awareness. This nonjudgment bit is also where we have an opportunity to break the binary of the Second Noble Truth, or at least loosen its grip a bit. Mindfulness invites us to stay watchful of the ways that we latch on to the sweet experiences and steamroll the less preferable ones. Herein lies the practice itself.

Catching Beauty in the Act

When it comes to practicing mindfulness on the path, I've heard it referred to as the spice that flavors all dishes; applying mindfulness to anything we engage in has the tendency to bring the flavor profile of our experience forward in a more visceral way. By engaging the five tiny touchstones of our senses in the present moment, we consciously become more sensitized, more available. We're able to squeeze more of the juice out of the moment because we're making direct contact with it. All day long we have access to a symphony of simple delights, and yet we're often so engrossed in our thoughts or fixated on achieving a peak experience of gratification that we completely miss out on the infinitesimal beauties that sprinkle the ordinary world. The practice of mindfulness on the path disrupts our habit of getting lost somewhere between our eyebrows and brings us back to a more awake, embodied, and available way of moving through the world. I've heard it said that "the devil is in the details," but I would venture to say that "the divine" can be found there too.

I often joke with my meditation students that I keep a journal called "Stuff Meditators Say." I'm frequently touched by the tiny pleasures that people experience in session and the nuanced descriptions that they share: the sunlight streaming in a staccato rhythm, warming the brick wall between clouds, or the gentle swoosh of leaves brushing against the skylight. I had a student describe staying watchful of even his physical pain. Rather than judging or rushing to shift it, he simply created space to allow it to evolve. Eventually he felt it dissolve into a warm and tender sensation that was more interesting and complex than the word "pain" could embody. *Hello, you nasty little hip-pain demon, reveal yourself to me.* The French philosopher Simone Weil writes that "attention is the rarest and purest form of generosity."[3] In the case of mindfulness on the path, attention is the generosity that we're extending to ourselves, all aspects of ourselves, by staying open to our experience. The dignity, worth, and beauty of our world is quietly announcing itself at all times. We just need to make ourselves available to catch it in the act.

The Four Foundations of Mindfulness

The roots of traditional mindfulness are plucked from the teachings of the Satipatthana Sutta, which details the Four Foundations of Mindfulness: mindfulness of body, emotions, mind, and phenomena. As with the meditation techniques described in this book, when it comes to practicing mindfulness the first step is to find a sturdy and sustainable seat. We can practice these foundations of mindfulness anywhere; however, it can be helpful to give ourselves a training ground where we won't be interrupted. This continuity is what makes formal meditation practice so valuable. In the same way that I find working from a dedicated work space considerably more conducive to doing good work than working from home with all of its distractions, creating a dedicated space for practicing mindfulness on the path while we develop our chops helps to facilitate a more natural and seamless spillover into our everyday lives.

Mindfulness of the Body

As Chögyam Trungpa once noted, "Mindfulness of body is connected with the earth. It is an openness that has a base, a foundation."[4] It's in this practice that we bring our full attention to our physical body as it's resting in space. While staying attuned to our somatic experience, we're also watchful of what our attention naturally picks up. This might mean feeling the weight of our body against the surface that we're on, the surface of the skin against the texture of our clothes, the temperature of the air. We might even find ourselves conducting a full-body scan, tracing our awareness in a slow and deliberate fashion, as though our awareness is magnetized to our skin, from the spaces between our toes up to the skin behind our ears and back down again, feeling into the quality of each space. Can we feel ourselves inside of our body here? There is something wildly sensual about mindfulness of the body practices in the most literal sense of the word; our senses are physically oriented, and being embodied in this way can activate our sensorial experience.

The true purpose with this foundation practice is to give ourselves an opportunity to fully arrive in our body and to stay for long enough to find our home here. Just this. Just this body here in space. Just this body here in space, breathing. This is not always easy. Especially if we have a complicated relationship with our body or if being in our body has historically felt unsafe. Again, the crux of this practice is to notice what arises as we feel our way into and through our body in a nonjudgmental way. Perhaps there is judgment, discomfort, or shame that comes through when we pay attention to our physical form. *Hello, you tender, nasty, shadowy bits. Thank you for the information.* Can we create space for these feelings to coexist? Do we feel safe enough to turn and look at our judgment, discomfort, or shame in a loving and reassuring way? We might even place a hand on our heart or belly and rest our attention in the rise and fall against the skin of our palms. This body is your home. Let it know that you are here for it and that you won't turn away.

Mindfulness of Emotions

It makes sense that mindfulness of emotions would fall on the heels of mindfulness of body. Emotions are both produced by and experienced inside the body, as a visceral sensation. This practice is our opportunity to slow things down enough to stay watchful, in real time, of our felt interior lives. After spending a few minutes with mindfulness of our body, we often begin to feel more connected, rooted, and present. Emotions might begin to naturally arise, just by merit of us slowing down enough to notice them. A lot tends to come up the moment we sit down. Perhaps we have undigested emotional material from the day that we haven't had space to truly feel. Perhaps there is a lingering mood or emotional flavor that is present, a quality of mind, so to speak. Perhaps there isn't much emotional material present at all. That's okay too. Making something happen is not the purpose of any mindfulness practice. We're simply staying open, receptive, and watchful of what already is. If we do this, we can turn our attention to our feeling state and just leave the door open for whatever naturally presents itself; as with inviting our demons to tea, we keep the door cracked open a bit with a welcome sign to sincerely greet whatever arrives.

Mindfulness of Mind

It also makes perfect sense that mindfulness of our mind would fall on the heels of mindfulness of emotions. When struck by an emotion inside of our body, the natural inclination for most of us is to simply pole-vault into thinking. We have a gorgeous, complex universe that lives between our eyebrows, and it's not uncommon for many of us to spend the bulk of our time up there. I certainly have had mornings when I got up with an alarm and immediately turned on my mental autopilot: Make coffee. Shower. Feed the dog. Ride the subway. Check my email. I arrive at my morning meeting before I'm clocked by the realization of *Wait . . . how did I even get here?* Chalk it up to spinning around in my little mind space, oblivious that I was lost in thought.

Mindfulness of mind is the practice of becoming very intimate and aware of the world up there in a moment-to-moment way. When we first begin to meditate it might feel like our mind is unusually busy, producing an impenetrable stream of thought. I once had a student describe becoming acquainted with her mind as like trying to take a sip from a gushing fire hose. The truth is that our mind was always this busy; we're just noticing it for the first time. Again, the nonjudgment piece of mindfulness as a practice encourages us to take a proverbial step back and to simply stay watchful without making our thoughts mean anything about us, one way or another.

One analogy that can be useful with this part of the practice is to keep the front and the back doors open. Whatever thoughts arise, we allow them to enter, pass on through, and leave without a fight. Just a thought. Allow it to go. We can loosen the self-identification a bit. Of course this is easier said than done. More often than not, mindfulness of mind gives us a clear and unadulterated view of how we judge nearly everything, including ourselves, on the binary that's reflected in the Second Noble Truth: Yes versus no. Good versus bad. Delicious versus disgusting. The crux of this practice is to see if we can loosen up a little bit and simply relax into our experience, while staying watchful of where our mind goes.

Mindfulness of Phenomena

Mindfulness of phenomena is the all-encompassing foundation of mindfulness that encourages us to pay attention to the Buddha's teachings as we engage in our everyday lives. What might it be like to bring the Four Noble Truths to mind in this very moment? How might keeping the Eightfold Path in mind inform my participation here? So many of us read a book on Buddhist teachings and then simply go about our lives. Only when something goes terribly wrong do we think, *What was that thing the Buddha said about suffering?* By becoming mindful of dharmas, or all phenomena, we are saying that whatever we encounter in our day-to-day experience, good or bad, can be brought to our spiritual path. This simple framework the Buddha provided for us is as applicable to modern living as it was 2,600 years ago when he introduced it. By continuing to contemplate and reflect on these teachings, we can learn to live a life of meaning.

On the Spot Practice

If your daily meditation practice has been at the 101 level, it's time to bring it to the 202 level. You don't have to become an "advanced" practitioner, but simply adding five to ten minutes to your daily mindfulness of breath practice can help keep the demons in check. Besides increasing the amount of time you meditate, take a few moments throughout the day to focus also on mindfulness of body; see if you can do on-the-spot mindfulness of emotions and mindfulness of mind practices, noticing when you are exposed to a demon of overwhelming emotion or distracting mind and coming back to what is happening right here and now, without judgment. At any point, you can apply mindfulness of phenomena—perhaps by recalling any one of the Four Noble Truths we've discussed here or by picking up a dharma book and opening to a random page. Remember the root teachings of the Buddha and see if they jog your memory, reminding you that this, too, shall pass, and that you are innately okay as you are.

Insight through Repetition

Beneficial Concentration

In the wholeheartedness of concentration, world and self
begin to cohere. With that state comes an enlarging:
of what may be known, what may be felt, what may be done.

Jane Hirshfield, *Nine Gates*

When I was a kid, we moved frequently and I often felt displaced. After one such move, my grandma gave my mother a
root as a housewarming gift. There was nothing special about
this root that sat on a living-room shelf, beyond that is was
a strange addition to our new apartment. It was roughly the
size of my palm, bulbous, and gnarled, with dirt caked in its
crevices. Small shoots reached out blindly for nourishment
in the way that antennae sprout from potatoes to scout for
soil when they've been forgotten in the crisper too long. As
a kid, the gift seemed odd, but now the root-as-metaphor
makes perfect sense to me. The root stands for stability and
sturdiness, a dedicated allegiance to the space one occupies.
A commitment to continue to burrow deeper where one is
planted so that the shoot aboveground can continue to unfurl,
rise, and bear fruit. The root is also an apt metaphor for the
unseen world of our interior life. Roots facilitate growth in

the form of what we interact with in the world by taking up space in the earth below.

On the Eightfold Path, Beneficial Concentration involves that which we bring our consistent attention to and the proverbial roots that we put down in that space as a result. We might also think about this part of our practice as Beneficial Effort Part II: The Long Game. This aspect of our path, where we work to establish our mind in a beneficial way, is foundational and ongoing. As the Eight Worldly Winds keep toppling us, leaving us unable to find the ground beneath our feet, Beneficial Concentration provides an antidote of sorts. We practice not only landing, but also putting down roots when we do land. In other words, we're talking about commitment. Signing up, and then showing up, day in and day out, even when the going gets tough.

Now, if your first impulse upon hearing *commitment* is to run for the hills, I admit that I'll be two steps behind you. Commitment takes sustained effort, and traditionally I've associated a lack of commitment with freedom. Who doesn't want to be able to change their mind on a whim and pivot life in any direction they please, with very little responsibility and few repercussions? I have a long history of lack of commitment in both my relationships and my work. Skimming the surface of things with no skin in the game. Changing the scenery when it no longer suited my fancy. This worked pretty well for me in the years when I was figuring things out (which never fully ends, if we're honoring the flux of things). When I first encountered the Buddhist concept of nonattachment, I scooped it up as validation that I could keep a cool remove from my life and pass it off as "wisdom." However, the appeal of staying unattached left the earth around me scorched and barren on a number of occasions. Dropped friendships. Discarded romances.

Half-baked aspirations that never fully formed. The irony is that my chronic fickleness didn't actually feel like freedom. It felt like a very lonely pattern that I was stuck in, one of setting fires and walking away. What I didn't understand until far into my twenties is that the beauty of commitment gives our lives a thread of continuity, a through line we can follow back to the light that's left on at home. Continuity is particularly useful on those dark nights of the soul. It reminds us of who we are and what we belong to because we know where we have been.

The crux of Beneficial Concentration is that it is a practice of deepening into a chosen area of commitment; this in turn trains our mind over time to continue to come back to what we have committed to. Putting down chosen roots, beneficial roots, and not just following the karma of habit energy isn't always easy. Again, concentration takes work. If you've ever experienced a bout of raging resistance, then you know what I mean. The Five Hindrances is a teaching that features a cameo of all of our favorite familiar demons, or hindrances. These hindrances have a well-timed way of stepping out of the dark to voice their objections whenever a new commitment needs our concentration in order to be fulfilled. The first hindrance is our old friend fixation: the desire for something different and shiny, the insistence on doing it perfectly. The moment that difficulty arises, she's here to remind you that there is something new (and obviously better) around the corner. In root-poison style, fixation is followed by the second hindrance, aversion. Aversion might show up as resentment, impatience, or avoidance of the task at hand. She procrastinates by folding her underwear instead. She gets angry at the person who made her do this task even though she obviously opted into it. The third hindrance to Beneficial Concentration is lethargy, laziness, when physical heaviness and mental sludge are par for the course. I equate this hindrance to the way a baby passes out when overstimulated. Sometimes our mind will simply shut down when we become overwhelmed or overcommitted. The fourth hindrance is speedy restlessness, an anxiety of body and mind that makes concentration all but impossible. Finally, there is our old friend doubt, preaching lack of conviction and trust. *Who do you think you are, anyway? You're never going to get it right, so why even bother?*

We see the raging resistance of the five hindrances in the story of Siddhartha Gautama; when he commits to awaken under the Bodhi tree he is confronted by the demons of his mind with Mara as the ringleader. I imagine all five of these slippery apparitions riding in on a steel chariot of resistance each time that we sit down to concentrate. There will always be demons making commitment challenging. Especially if the task at hand is something that is close to our heart or requires us to put skin in the game.

The evening that my husband proposed to me, we came home and called our mothers to share the good news with them. His mother's response to our engagement is my favorite because of her delightful honesty. "You're engaged? To each other?" she asked. "Wonderful. You're both so brave!" Given that there is a statistical likelihood that our marriage will end in divorce, she wasn't wrong. We are brave. The First Noble Truth reminds us that the best-case scenario is that we're in love until one of us dies. Any time we commit to something that is unknown, is difficult, or has potential repercussions, we are exercising a courage of sorts. And if we're aware of the truth of impermanence, we're doubling down on our risk. Even our commitments are temporary. All that we love, we lose.

When it comes to Beneficial Concentration, it's helpful to remember the interlocking nature of the Eightfold Path. None of its aspects happen in a vacuum; they work in concert to support one another. The path of awakening is holistic in nature. Beneficial View can come in handy by helping us investigate our narratives around loss, uncertainty, and commitment. If I screw this up, does that then mean I am a screwup? Inherently and at my core? The more that we practice familiarizing ourselves with the views and narratives that obscure our self-worth, the more those demons lose authority over our choices. Beneficial Intention reminds us why we've committed in the first place, keeping the yes of our commitment fresh. Beneficial Effort helps us protect our practice out of reverence for the commitment we've made to ourselves. The practice of Beneficial Concentration within the Eightfold Path ensures that not only are we able to hold our seat, but that we've also developed sturdy roots beneath it that keep us anchored to our path.

The Reciprocity In Between

The American poet Peggy Freydberg began composing poetry when she was in her nineties. She had always been immersed in the world of literature and editing; her friends were members of the East Coast literary world, and both of her husbands were in publishing. Literature was Mrs. Freydberg's orientation to the world; it was where her roots were. Though the world didn't see the foliage of what had been planted and nurtured until the final years of her life, her gorgeous collection *Poems from the Pond* had been undoubtedly percolating in her unseen world for decades before blossoming fully. The poem "Survival of the Fittest" is a rich contemplation of her relationship with the lilac bushes outside her home. The opening line reads, "I like to think that it matters to the lilac that my face is thrust into its gloss of heaven."[1]

I love this poem and this line for so many reasons. They give me the image of Peggy Freydberg thrusting her weathered face into the lilac bushes every single spring for decades as ritual act, as a through line of continuity in her life. They cause me to imagine the rush of ninety years of seasonal memories that this "gloss of heaven" must have evoked for her. Mostly I love how they express the intimate relationship she had with her lilacs. There is a sense, having returned to them year after year after year, that the relationship is not one sided. The lilacs are equally involved in this exchange, and both lilacs and Mrs. Freydberg seem to pick up where they left off. A persuasive exchange occurs between the two of them, one involving the fidelity of bliss.

One of the hallmarks of Beneficial Concentration is that when we commit our attentiveness over a sustained period of time, what we commit to inevitably commits back. In the suttas, the cornerstone of Beneficial Concentration is *jhana*, which refers to a state of complete mental absorption. According to the suttas, there are four jhanas, along with four immaterial states of mind. Together they are often talked about as the eight expanding states of concentration that one can reach through meditation practice. The development of these states of concentration reminds me of the way a root grows. An offshoot of the root develops to soak up more minerals, and as this side tendril grows, it generates yet another spindly offshoot, each new appendage of the root reaching infinitely further into the soil, fastening the entire plant more firmly into the earth while soaking in nutrients. Considering Beneficial Concentration as absorbed concentration in this way implies that there is an exchange taking place—a taking in, an integration, a digestion. Not only are we committing to our object of concentration, but we are also making ourselves available to be changed by it, shaped by it in the same way that Peggy Freydberg's exchange with her lilacs persuaded her to shift her view.

I've seen this exchange occur with people who have a concentration practice of any kind. Interestingly, when choosing a major to study during university or college, it's sometimes called choosing your *concentration*. During my time at art school my mind was absorbed by design. I had a sketch teacher who made it clear that her role was to teach us how to see the human body through a more mathematical lens. We dissected ratios of the face and proportions of the physique. We sketched the triangles of the body and the way that muscle groups contract and lengthen in opposition. That period of concentration, hours spent poorly sketching ovals and angles and the slight changes of the body along its axis brought forth by different poses, made me cry tears of frustration, because my sketches were crap, and I just didn't get it. I just couldn't see. Until the day that I did. I haven't sketched in over a decade, but I still remember how to "see," thanks to that extended concentration. The exchange of my hours spent in frustration for the ability to see the world differently overall was simply invaluable.

This type of immersion invites our object of concentration to reveal itself to us, sometimes incrementally, sometimes all at once. It can be a bit of an endurance test, but we're ultimately rewarded with ever-deepening insight into the nature of the thing. You can see this interplay in people who love to cook; their view becomes oriented to food. The same is true with musicians, who hear the musicality in everything, and mathematicians, who see the geometry of the world. There is a knowingness that develops through commitment that is different from just simply having surface-level and conceptual information. Insight that's developed through repetition is

Beneficial Concentration at its finest. Wisdom that's experiential. Knowledge that's baked in the bones.

Adopting Self-Worth as Our Concentration

Beneficial Concentration is about putting down roots and committing and then watching what we commit to reveal itself to us. This can only happen in intimate relationships. It's also about the practice of mental absorption on the meditation cushion, for which there is no substitute. The ordinary magic of sitting practice is that as we steady the body, the mind is apt to follow. We're creating space for the mind to spin, raise a ruckus, and rage until it tires itself out on its own and goes to lie peacefully in the shade of large sturdy tree. Meditation is the training ground where we learn how to unify the mind, harmonize what is fragmented, and stop the war that we wage with ourselves.

A colleague of mine, who is a childhood psychologist, has a wonderful exercise that she uses with children to help them understand the mind and meditation. She gives each child a mason jar filled with water and glitter and has them move around the room. Their jars inevitably get shaken, no matter how careful their movement, sending clouds of glitter swirling through their jars. She then invites them to take a seat and rest and watch while the glitter settles to the bottom. Each movement sends up glitter. Each moment of stillness allows the water to clear. And so it is with attempting to concentrate and settle our mind.

To concentrate something is to distill it down to its essential matter. It's the process of reducing it over a period of time so that anything that is not that thing boils off, and what remains is the essence itself. In the same way, the process and the path of revealing our self-worth are a distillation of sorts. As we peel back what is irrelevant and encounter our unseen world, we begin to befriend what has been discarded. The demon material that guards our worth gets invited to be seen and heard.

There are three forms of concentration that we can employ on the path to self-worth. The first is the concentration of study. This is how the insight of understanding develops within us. Going back to the relationship between view and practice, study is how our view develops, such as by reading books, listening to talks, and coming to understand these teachings through a variety of different perspectives. The second concentration is that of contemplation. This is how the insight of experience develops. Contemplation asks us to take our studies out into the world and to notice how the teachings interact with our own direct and lived experience. The third concentration is that of meditation practice. This is how the insight of realization develops. We can never complete the path of self-worth, but the good news is that we are already complete—not demons aside, but demons included.

On the Spot Practice Open your front door and let into your home whatever demon has been trying to nudge its way in. In other words, take some time to acknowledge your self-doubt, anxiety, and fear—all of it. Make some tea. Pour it. Sit down and imagine you are sitting across from your demon. It's a part of you but you're looking right at it. Hold your seat. See if any valid communication bubbles up from it. Smile. Know that in this very moment, you are okay.

Conclusion

Roshi Joan Halifax, the abbot of the Upaya Institute and Zen Center in Santa Fe, New Mexico, refers to a "blue-collar Buddhism." I quite like the folksy, hardworking, salt-of-the-earth quality of this term, which invites us to roll up our sleeves and get our hands dirty, to work with the contents of our lives, as they are. Up close and intimately. It invites us to get close to the earth. To fall to our knees and put our hands in the mud pit. To smell its loamy, fertile quality. To recognize that the soil of our lives is workable and to stop trying to transcend its messy and ordinary bits.

Acknowledging that the totality of our messy, ordinary, fragile human life has intrinsic dignity is where the good stuff happens and is how we feel our worth. Demons, confusion, neurosis, wisdom, clarity, sanity, and all. We are both unfolding potential and already complete; we are basically good and fundamentally whole. Remembering and relaxing into these realizations against the backdrop of a culture that profits from self-doubt, of course, takes practice. Much like the nemesis principle, the moment that we illuminate our worth, its shadow stands out in sharp relief. The allegory of inviting our demons to tea suggests that we don't ignore the dodgy parts; rather we learn how to work with them, skillfully and directly. Facing the entirety of who we are is the path of practicing our worth.

The cornerstone of this practice is meditation. When you first launch a meditation practice, you're taking a front-row seat to your own mind. This has the potential to be an intimate discovery of everything that lives inside: our demons, our wisdom, our inherited narratives, our impulses, and our habits. My advice is to approach yourself with care. The best antidote to feeling that our worth is conditional is the practice of offering ourselves unconditional kindness. Day in and day out. Over and over. Like butter and wax, our hearts soften when warmth is applied, as do our rigid standards and impossible expectations of ourselves. Meditation practice is also our training ground for learning how to hold our seats. We're training in softening, but also in sturdiness, taking up space without apology or armor. We allow the earth to hold us and bear witness to our worth, as we bear witness to ourselves. Feeling the body breathing reminds us of our inherent intelligence and belonging. This is happening and it's happening now, without being instructed or asked. In meditation we're sensitizing ourselves to the infinitesimal beauty that can only be appreciated when we're available to this singular moment.

The Four Noble Truths illuminate what we're encountering in our meditation practice and in our experience of being human. The First Noble Truth confirms that being a human is hard and that pain and discomfort are a part of the landscape. By reminding us that we're not alone, it's also a window into how we can develop empathy and compassion. The Second Noble Truth highlights how we struggle against our condition by trying to snuff out discomfort with pleasure. This is the breeding ground for the confusion of our mind that hijacks our inherent wakefulness; the sneaky little demons of greed, fixation, grasping, comparison, judgment, and aggression all rise to the occasion when we refuse to meet and make room for our experience as it is. They show up in the most mundane circumstances. *Hello, you beautiful nasty beasts.* Meditation helps us to identify our difficult emotions and confused states of mind and to welcome them in, without giving them carte blanche to take the keys or run the show. We widen our capacity to accept ourselves and accommodate our conditions by inviting our demons for tea. The cycle of the Three Root Poisons of attachment, aggression, and ignorance begins to soften when we remember that our identity is not fixed and our worth is not conditional; we are not the transient states that we tend to identify with. Status, gain, pleasure, and praise all feel wonderful, but they are conditional and bound to change.

The Third Noble Truth introduces us to the possibility of healing the cycle of the root poisons, and the Fourth Noble Truth presents a new option by offering us the Eightfold Path, a holistic, nonlinear, moment-to-moment way of cultivating the dignity of our life and of realizing our inherent enoughness. Together it is a complete path of looking at and addressing our demons, sharing tea with them, and moving into a life marked by wakefulness, joy, and meaning. To some extent we all have an interior editor—that voice inside that is critical, spiteful, and unkind. The good news is that you are not alone and that internal voice doesn't have to be a problem. *Wholeness* means "the entirety," and we are whole enough to include it all.

Acknowledgments

Thank you to everyone at the Sounds True family who has touched this book, from proposal to print, and brought it to fruition. I realize that I will never meet many of you, though your contribution is deeply felt. It takes a village, and I have tremendous appreciation for the soil that your particular village is built on. Special thanks to the editing team, Leslie Brown, James Lainsbury, and, of course, Gretel Hakanson, for helping me heave this manuscript over every deadline, often in the final hour. I cannot thank you enough for your patience and discernment. Also to Jennifer Brown for scooping this book up under your wing and giving it your care and direction in its early stages. Your generosity has been invaluable.

To Lodro Rinzler, my husband, my champion, and my extra set of eyes. Thank you for being the John to my Joan. I adore you and I am unbelievably lucky for your love. Special thanks to Marisa Viola for loaning me your steadfast support and prismatic mind, and for driving across the country with me to realize this book idea. You are the definition of ride or die. Thank you to my mom, Lisa Limbach, for the day spent on your back porch talking this book into being. Your love and support along the way have been indispensable. Thank you to my dad, Angelo Santilli, for your enduring belief in everything I do; your faith in me is a rare gift. To Ralph De La Rosa and Kate Johnson, thank you for supporting my process during your own book-writing processes, because teamwork makes the dream work. Beth Rinzler, I feel so lucky that you are my mother-friend-in-law; thank you for being the consummate retreat master and for opening your doors repeatedly during this process. I could not have finished this book without your generosity. Special thanks to Haley Schwartz, for your soothsaying and encouragement; to Christina Fewerda, for the work dates; and to all my friends and family members who have cheered this book on and waited patiently for me to return your calls, emails, and texts.

I owe an incredible debt of gratitude to my teachers and *kalyanamitras* along the way, namely Mr. Tim Siebert, James Price, Denis Cicero, Ethan Nichtern, Susan Piver, and the Venerable Robina Courtin; you have been formative to my experience and I am eternally grateful for your influence. Thank you to the dozens of people who shared their stories of self-worth during my research process. You are seen and loved and woven into the fabric of these pages. To all of the delivery people who fed me dinner as I wrote, and to the numerous more whom I didn't mention by name: thank you, thank you, thank you. May it be of benefit.

Notes

Chapter 5. How to Hold Your Seat

1. Herbert Benson and Miriam Z. Klipper, *The Relaxation Response* (New York: Morrow, 1976).

Chapter 6. Restless Everything Syndrome: The First Noble Truth

1. Chögyam Trungpa, *Meditation in Action*, 40th anniversary ed. (Boston: Shambhala Publications, 2010), 15.
2. David Chadwick, *Crooked Cucumber: The Life and Zen Teaching of Shunryu Suzuki* (New York: Broadway Books, 1999), xii.
3. Raquel Tibol, *Frida Kahlo: An Open Life*, trans. Elinor Randall (Albuquerque: University of New Mexico Press, 2000), 28.
4. Shunryu Suzuki, *Zen Mind, Beginner's Mind*, Shambhala Library ed. (Boston: Shambhala Publications, 2006), 28.
5. Thanissaro Bhikkhu, trans., "Kisagotami Theri" (Thig 10), Access to Insight: Readings in Theravada Buddhism (BCBS edition), last modified November 30, 2013, accesstoinsight. org/tipitaka/kn/thig/thig.10.01.than.html.
6. Naomi Shihab Nye, "Kindness," in *Words Under the Words: Selected Poems* (Portland, OR: Eighth Mountain Press, 1995), 42.
7. Chögyam Trungpa, *Shambhala: The Sacred Path of the Warrior*, 1st ed. (Boston: Shambhala Publications, 1984), 34.

Chapter 7. Welcome to the Charnel Grounds: The Second Noble Truth

1. *Willy Wonka & the Chocolate Factory*, directed by Mel Stuart, written by Roald Dahl (United States: Wolper Pictures, The Quaker Oats Company; Distribution, Paramount Pictures, June 30, 1971), film, 1 hour, 40 min.
2. Ralph Waldo Emerson, *Essays and English Traits* (New York: P. F. Collier, 1910), 310.
3. Simon Sinek, *Leaders Eat Last: Why Some Teams Pull Together and Others Don't* (New York: Penguin, 2014), 63, 87, 232.
4. Robina Courtin, "Awakening Our Hearts in the World—Part 1 of 2," recorded September 19, 2012, at The Interdependence Project, New York, NY, audio, 1:06:08, media.theidproject.org/media/podcast/ven-robin-courtin-awakening-our-hearts-world-part-1-2.
5. Robina Courtin, "Awakening Our Hearts in the World."
6. Joan Didion, *Slouching Towards Bethlehem: Essays* (New York: Farrar, Straus, and Giroux, 2008), 145.
7. Thanissaro Bhikkhu, trans., "Lokavipatti Sutta: The Failings of the World" (AN 8.6), Access to Insight: Readings in Theravada Buddhism (BCBS edition), last modified July 4, 2010, accesstoinsight.org/tipitaka/an/an08/an08.006.than.html.

Chapter 8. Pure Potential and the Cessation of Suffering: The Third Noble Truth

1. James Baldwin, interview by Jane Howard, "Telling Talk from a Negro Writer," *LIFE Magazine* 54, no. 21 (May 24, 1963), 89.
2. Thanissaro Bhikkhu, trans., "Maha-mangala Sutta: Protection" (Sn 2.4), Access to Insight: Readings in Theravada Buddhism (BCBS edition), last modified November 30, 2013, accesstoinsight.org/tipitaka/kn/snp/snp.2.04.than.html.
3. Lewis Carroll, *Alice's Adventures in Wonderland* (New York: Macmillan, 1920), 60.
4. Alexander Harris, "U.S. Self Storage Industry Statistics," SpareFoot Storage Beat, updated March 21, 2018, sparefoot.com/self-storage/news/1432-self-storage-industry-statistics.

5. Meghan Henry et al. for The U.S. Department of Housing and Urban Development, Office of Community Planning and Development, "Part 1: Point-in-Time Estimates of Homelessness," in *The 2017 Annual Homeless Assessment Report (AHAR) to Congress (December 2017)*, hudexchange. info/resources/documents/2017-AHAR-Part-1.pdf.

Chapter 9. Surrendering the Plan, Walking the Path: The Fourth Noble Truth

1. Twyla Tharp, *The Creative Habit: Learn It and Use It for Life*, 1st ed. (New York: Simon and Schuster, 2003), 10.

Chapter 10. What's the Story, Morning Glory? Beneficial View

1. Joan Didion, *The White Album*, 1st ed. (New York: Simon and Schuster, 1979), 1.

2. Lynn Twist, *The Soul of Money: Transforming Your Relationship with Money and Life*, 1st ed. (New York: W. W. Norton, 2003), 44.

Chapter 12. Mind Meets World: Beneficial Communication

1. Albert Mehrabian and Morton Wiener, "Decoding of Inconsistent Communications," *Journal of Personality and Social Psychology* 6, no. 1 (May 1967): 109–114, doi.org/10.1037/h0024532; Albert Mehrabian and Susan R. Ferris, "Inference of Attitudes from Nonverbal Communication in Two Channels," *Journal of Consulting Psychology* 31, no. 3 (June 1967): 248–252, doi.org/10.1037/h0024648.

2. Thanissaro Bhikkhu, trans., "Vacca Sutta: A Statement" (AN 5.198), Access to Insight: Readings in Theravada Buddhism (BCBS edition), last modified July 3, 2010, accesstoinsight.org/tipitaka/an/an05/an05.198.than.html.

3. Van Jones, *Beyond the Messy Truth: How We Came Apart, How We Come Together*, repr. ed. (New York: Ballantine Books, 2018), 56.

4. Thich Nhat Hanh, *How to Love*, repr. ed. (Berkeley, CA: Parallax Press, 2014), 3.

Chapter 13. Karma Made Me Do It: Beneficial Action

1. *The Lone Ranger*, season 4, episode 39, "Heart of a Cheater," directed by Wilhelm Thiele, written by George W. Trendle, Bert Lambert, and Fran Striker, aired June 9, 1955, on ABC.
2. Henry Miller, *Henry Miller on Writing*, comp. Thomas H. Moore (New York: New Directions Publishing, 1964), 25.

Chapter 14. Work, Money, Purpose: Beneficial Livelihood

1. Thanissaro Bhikkhu, trans., "Magga-vibhanga Sutta: An Analysis of the Path" (SN 45.8), Access to Insight: Readings in Theravada Buddhism (BCBS edition), last modified November 30, 2013, accesstoinsight.org/tipitaka/sn/sn45/sn45.008.than.html.
2. Thanissaro Bhikkhu, trans., "Samaññaphala Sutta: The Fruits of the Contemplative Life" (DN 2), Access to Insight: Readings in Theravada Buddhism (BCBS edition), last modified November 30, 2013, accesstoinsight.org/tipitaka/dn/dn.02.0.than.html.
3. *Mad Men*, season 3, episode 11, "The Gypsy and the Hobo," directed by Jennifer Getzinger, written by Matthew Weiner, Marti Noxon, Cathryn Humphris, and Kater Gordon, aired October 25, 2009, on AMC.
4. Narada Thera, trans., "Dighajanu (Vyagghapajja) Sutta: Conditions of Welfare" (AN 8.54), Access to Insight: Readings in Theravada Buddhism (BCBS edition), last modified November 30, 2013, accesstoinsight.org/tipitaka/an/an08/an08.054.nara.html.

Chapter 15. Accounting for Our Energy: Beneficial Effort

1. Thich Nhat Hanh and Lilian W. Y. Cheung, *Savor: Mindful Eating, Mindful Life*, 1st ed. (New York: HarperCollins, 2010), 15.

Chapter 16. The Spice That Flavors All Dishes: Beneficial Mindfulness

1. Adrienne A. Taren, J. David Creswell, and Peter J. Gianaros, "Dispositional Mindfulness Co-Varies with Smaller Amygdala and Caudate Volumes in Community Adults," *PLOS One* (May 22, 2013), doi.org/10.1371/journal. pone.0064574; Daniel Reed, "Sahaja Yoga Meditation Increases Gray Matter in the Brain, Study Finds," PsyPost, September 11, 2016, psypost.org/2016/09/sahaja-yoga-meditation-increases-gray-matter-brain-study-finds-44886.
2. *Mindful* staff, "Jon Kabat-Zinn: Defining Mindfulness," *Mindful*, January 11, 2017, mindful.org/ jon-kabat-zinn-defining-mindfulness.
3. Miklos Vetö, *The Religious Metaphysics of Simone Weil*, trans. Joan Dargan, SUNY Series, Simone Weil Studies (Albany, NY: State University of New York Press, 1994), 45.
4. Chögyam Trungpa, *The Heart of the Buddha*, 1st ed. (Boston: Shambhala Publications, 1991), 25.

Chapter 17. Insight Through Repetition: Beneficial Concentration

1. Margaret Howe Freydberg, *Poems from the Pond: 107 Years of Words and Wisdom, the Writings of Peggy Freydberg*, ed. Laurie David (Pasadena, CA: Hybrid Nation, 2015), 75.

About the Author

Adreanna Limbach is the head teacher at MNDFL meditation studios and a personal development coach who helps women access their inherent clarity and confidence so that they can expand their freedom in business and life. She's practiced meditation for the last twenty years and has taught Buddhist studies, meditation, and the cultivation of self-worth since 2012 at locations across the globe.

She has spent a decade mentoring do-gooders at the Institute for Integrative Nutrition as a coach, and she has catalyzed cohorts of tomorrow's leaders around social change as an executive coach and faculty member at the Institute for Compassion Leadership. Her work has been featured by the *New York Times*, Refinery29, *Women's Health*, and xoJane. She lives with her husband and too many small animals in an apartment in NYC. You can find out more at AdreannaLimbach.com.

About Sounds True

Sounds True is a multimedia publisher whose mission is to inspire and support personal transformation and spiritual awakening. Founded in 1985 and located in Boulder, Colorado, we work with many of the leading spiritual teachers, thinkers, healers, and visionary artists of our time. We strive with every title to preserve the essential "living wisdom" of the author or artist. It is our goal to create products that not only provide information to a reader or listener, but that also embody the quality of a wisdom transmission.

For those seeking genuine transformation, Sounds True is your trusted partner. At SoundsTrue.com you will find a wealth of free resources to support your journey, including exclusive weekly audio interviews, free downloads, interactive learning tools, and other special savings on all our titles.

To learn more, please visit SoundsTrue.com/freegifts or call us toll-free at 800.333.9185.